DIE IN THE
SANCTUARY

A STORY OF LOVE, LOSS, MISSION, AND UNSHAKEABLE FAITH

by

Sam Parsons

Published in Pasadena, CA, by Fireproof Ministries. Fireproof Ministries titles may be purchased in bulk for educational, business, fund-raising, or sales promotional use. For information, please e-mail info@fireproofministries.com

Unless otherwise noted, Scriptures are taken from the New American Standard Bible

The Library of Congress Cataloging-in-Publication **Data is on file with the Library of Congress** *ISBN-13: 978-0-578-52607-2*

DEDICATION

This book is dedicated to the memory of Colleen Parsons, who was always a lady. She changed my life in a million ways. She loved me, unconditionally, and was my inspiration, my best friend, my lover, and my soul-mate. She was the mother of my children, a great mom, and a loyal friend. She will always remain the one true love of my life, forever and ever, amen.

"An excellent wife is the crown of her husband,"

Proverbs 12:4a

"Her children rise up and bless her;
Her husband also, and he praises her, saying:
29 "Many daughters have done nobly,
But you excel them all."
30 Charm is deceitful and beauty is vain,
But a woman who fears the LORD, she shall be praised."

Proverbs 31:27-30

ACKNOWLEDGMENT

I am deeply grateful to all the family and friends who spoke into Colleen's and my life over the years and to those who encouraged me to write this book. It was written through many tears as I relived mine and Colleen's life together. I especially owe a debt of thanks to Craig and Jeanette Gross for encouraging me all along the way, and without their help, this book would not have come to be. My ultimate thanks go to God our Father who orchestrated so beautifully our life together and who remains faithful to His promises.

CHAPTER 1

I never thought this day would come.

I always thought I would be first.

The place was packed with old friends and family, almost standing room only. Under any other circumstances I would have been excited to see everyone, and I guess I still was, though not in a typical way. I was excited to see that so many people were showing love and all of it was being poured out on our family.

But oh, how I had dreaded this day.

My daughter had planned everything down to the last detail; all I had to do was show up and hopefully be able to say a few words about the person I had loved so deeply and had lost so suddenly. On the way to the church, I thought about running away—just hopping on a plane and flying to God knows where. I decided instead to buy a couple dozen helium balloons. Why I did that, I'll never really know for sure. I think I did it for the grandchildren to release after the crowd had gone home.

At any rate, here I was, crying my eyes out with a car full of balloons, trying to gain some composure. Everyone had been so lovely to me and warm and caring, and although I knew everyone had a pure heart about it, I was still sick of hearing, "She's in a better place." I knew they meant well.

But the better place, I kept thinking, *is here with me.*

I knew if anyone deserved to be in God's presence it was my girl. She had finished well and had done exceedingly beautiful things in her life. She had been a great wife and mother. She was perfect!

But she was gone.

It was like a terrible nightmare that wouldn't end. I couldn't get my head around the fact she was gone and not coming back.

I still struggle with it as I write this, although I trust God and believe He knows best for all concerned. That, however, was not my first thought. I have had to search for His purpose in all of it. I'm a bit better now; it has been a sincere search for peace. He is my comfort.

Let me tell you about my wife. Let me tell you about Colleen. Just talking about her sometimes helps me cope with the high waves of sorrow I experience daily.

About six or seven years ago, I came home only to be greeted by Colleen, and from the look on her face, I knew she'd done one of her rashly generous things. She was famous for them. She was a giver from the word "go." I mean, she'd give you the last dime she had. She was the most honest and giving person I ever met.

Here's an example, different from the one I'm about to tell you: one day shortly after Colleen and I were married, I came home and discovered all the furniture in the driveway. The couches, the chairs, the dining room table, the lamps—everything. I'd been a vagabond musician for a lot of my early years and had never had a lot of beautiful furniture, so when I married Colleen I acquired a bunch of furniture, and I thought we were rich.

But now all that beautiful furniture was outside of the house rather than inside, where it belonged. And my first thought wasn't, *What is my crazy wife doing?* Nor was it, *Did Colleen find some money to have the carpets cleaned?* Nor was it, *Fleas? Do we have fleas?*

No, my first thought was to take in the scene, notice the sectional, and think, *How did she get this couch out of the door?*

So I went inside and said, "What's going on? Why is all the furniture in the driveway?"

And Colleen said, "Well, there's an old missionary couple that just came off the mission field, and they found an apartment, but it's unfurnished, and they didn't have any furniture. So I gave them mine."

Of course, she did.

"Well, what are we going to do for furniture?" I asked.

"This furniture was my furniture," she said. "I don't want *my* furniture. I want *our* furniture. We're one now. I want our stuff."

I was too practical at that time in life to see the sweetness of her desire. "So where are we going to get our stuff?" I asked.

"We'll go to garage sales and things like that," she said. "We'll find it, or you can build it. If we need tables, you can make them."

"I don't know how to make stuff!"

"You can fix anything," she said. "You'll figure it out. But these people need help, and we don't need this. We're fine."

I stood there stunned. And also madly in love.

"I kept the mattress," she said, "and I kept Tasha's bedroom set, so we're good. It'll be good."

That wasn't the last time she gave away furniture, either. Years later, our sons Nick and Travis formed a band. They were probably around ten and 12 at the time, and they practiced in the garage, with Nick on guitar, Travis on drums, and a couple of neighbor kids on harmonica and bass.

It wasn't heavy metal or anything; it was just plain old rock and roll. But we lived in the middle of a cul-de-sac, and this guy across the street kept complaining every time they practiced. He even began yelling across the street at them and all kinds of stuff. So I hung a tarp inside the garage door, put lights up for them, and told them to play with the garage door closed, but he still complained.

One day in the middle of a rehearsal there was a knock on the garage door. Nick opened the door, and there were the cops!

"You have to stop playing, you're getting noise complaints," they said.

So I came home one day to find all our furniture in our living room was gone. When I left that morning it was there; when I came back, it was not.

Our family had the whole house, but Colleen had one room:

our front room, with white brocade chairs and a nice couch and a coffee table and a couple of lamps. It was the room we never went into, the one that was almost taboo. Almost like in the fifties when they put the plastic over the furniture. She wanted one clean, nice room, always ready and available in case guests would come over.

All of that nice furniture? Gone.

She'd given it away.

Instead, my old sound system was set up in there, along with a keyboard, a drum set, a guitar amp, and some microphones.

"This is no longer the living room," Colleen told me. "This is our music room. No one can complain about what we're doing inside our house. They're not going to tell us what we're going to do in our home."

And that was that. She gave away everything, and that was the music room, and that was where my kids' band rehearsed. It stayed that way for two or three years.

Now back to the time a few years ago when I came home to another surprise giveaway. But this time, though I didn't know it then, Colleen was giving something to me.

She greeted me as soon as I walked in the door.

"Honey," she said, "I have to tell you something I did."

"What did you do?"

"I canceled my life insurance."

We had something like a $25,000 life insurance policy on her at the time.

"You did what?"

"I canceled my life insurance policy," she calmly repeated.

"Why did you do that?"

"Well, I've been praying about it," she said, "and I thought about it, and if you had $25,000 if I died, then you would probably cry and cry and cry and never go back to work. But if you didn't have that money, then you would have to go back to work. You wouldn't have time to cry; you wouldn't have a chance to cry—you would just go on. You would mourn, and I'm sure you will, but you would be okay. But if you had that money, then you might not be okay, so I canceled it."

At the time, I was fit to be tied, but that's the way she thought.

She was actually looking out for me.

She knew me like a book.

She knew me inside and out.

She knew what I needed before I ever did.

As I write this to you, six weeks ago my wife breathed her last breath on this earth. This story is true and factual to the best of my memory, and I know I will have probably left a lot of it out, because after 34 years of life together every day, holding hands and the intimacies of walking through every one of life's challenges...we spent our time together. But it becomes surreal. I can't begin to express the depths of my sorrow and my loss of Colleen's company, and the writing of this story is one of the hardest things I've ever done.

I'm hoping that God receives glory for our life together and that my wife will be honored for the godly wife and woman she was. Mother and friend.

She died of sepsis.

We were on vacation, visiting our son in Tulsa, Oklahoma before going down to Texas, to the ranch where I grew up, just south of Waco.

We had a great time on our trip; we laughed and joked and

ate things we weren't supposed to (everything in the south is fried, it seems like).

And then she got sick on a Wednesday morning. By Wednesday night, I took her to the emergency room; then we rushed her to Waco, to the ICU at Providence Hospital.

Two weeks after that, she breathed her last breath.

She was only 61, and we thought we had twenty more years together.

But God had a different plan.

Now, six weeks later as I write this, I have just returned from a visit to an oncologist, where just this afternoon he informed me that I have stage-four pancreatic cancer and only a few weeks to live myself. So as love stories go, ours will continue in heaven.

For now, it's time to go to work.

CHAPTER 2

Before we go much further, I'll tell you a little bit of my story, give you the background on me so you can more fully understand my relationship with Colleen.

I spent much of my childhood on a ranch in Texas with my grandparents. My dad and I never got along very well; he had a little rage-aholic kind of thing that would show up when he'd get his temper up, and I seemed to push those buttons a lot.

I was always in trouble, and though my dad never would hit any of my three sisters or my mom, he didn't have any problem hitting a boy—so I took the brunt of his anger.

After I took a beating or two, my mom would send me home to the ranch, to my grandparents' house. This happened so often that I was raised part-time there on that Texas ranch. It didn't take me long to realize every time I'd go back to the house—and my dad—that I'd have to take a real good whipping until my mom would send me back to the ranch. So I liked it on the ranch.

When I got to be about twelve or thirteen years old, I started playing the guitar. My dad played too, so I thought maybe if I picked it up I could impress him, that he'd be so impressed by my playing that we'd have a close relationship. But I started getting pretty good, and my dad seemed to get jealous of that.

Later I think he took pride in it, but at the time, he didn't.

And so that made us even more distant; it gave him another reason to get mad at me.

You can probably figure out this next part. It's the kind of thing you've heard a million times already. I got good enough at guitar that I started playing in nightclubs when I was fourteen years old. Of course, I had a fake ID to get in, but that's how I worked my way through high school. After I graduated, I left home and started chasing a record career and stardom.

Of course, I played around with drugs, because that was the thing way back in the sixties and seventies, and when you're around that kind of culture, you can get caught up in it. Just starting in those first places, I'd play for ten dollars a night and all the chili I could eat and all the coffee I could drink...and then someone would always give me marijuana.

It was in one of these nightclubs where my life changed completely, though I didn't know it at the time. It was the spring of 1971, and it involved an old Irish beer-drinking buddy of mine who used to come to a supper club where I sang in Costa Mesa, California. He'd come in two or three times a week, and I would sit and visit with him in between sets. He was a truck driver, and since my dad had also been a truck driver, we understood each other and got along great. He seemed like a happy-go-lucky guy, and I liked him a lot.

One night he decided to bring in his three beautiful daughters with him, and though they were all beautiful young women, one, in particular, caught my eye.

Her name was Colleen McCune, and she would eventually be the love of my life.

I'd never seen anyone so beautiful. I can't emphasize that too strongly; I'll always remember that first vision of Colleen. Unfortunately, she was a little too young to date just then, but I remembered her, and she stayed in my mind long after they'd gone home for the evening.

I didn't interact with her that much back then, but I looked forward to seeing her every time she came in with her dad, which only happened a couple more times before my career started taking off.

It wouldn't be entirely honest for me to say I only had eyes for Colleen back then. I was just a year into this attempt at a music career when I met a girl who had been a grade behind me in high school; she graduated and then she and I went to college together and dated for a couple of years.

And then I asked her to marry me.

Why? Well, I was starving, not making any money in a small

college town. There wasn't any work. And so I was dirt-poor and hungry. Then I got a chance to go on the road with a band, and they were going to pay good money, as well as pay my room and board. I had to take the gig, but I didn't want to leave this girl behind, so: she and I ran off and got married.

It was probably the stupidest thing she's ever done. She was a straight-A student, and I was barely getting by with Cs. I didn't like college anyways; I only loved being with this girl. So we started this whirlwind, crazy-kid, hippie relationship that messed us both up. She was a good girl, a nice girl, but chasing after the music and the recording career, I started neglecting her. I wanted to pursue that brass ring. It was not a good situation: we were hippies from the sixties and screwed-up seventies, and my music career—not my marriage— was my biggest chase.

That chase was rewarded in 1972 when I landed a record contract with ABC records. It was a good record deal—I mean good as far as I had money. I did an album on ABC and got a big hit on Billboard and a big hit on Bill Gavin sheet, which was an accomplishment at the time. I was going to be the new hot artist; it looked like it was going well. My record was doing fine, and my touring schedule was lining up, too: I had six weeks booked with The Doobie Brothers and another six weeks booked with The Eagles.

They wouldn't have called it "unplugged" back then, but we were planning to do an unplugged tour, with me as the opening act, and everything was falling into place for it to go well. And then right at the last second, ABC Records pulled the plug on our unplugged tour! ABC Network ruled the nest at the time, and they had decided to fire all the higher-ups at ABC Records. When that happens in show business, any act that was on the roster at the time gets put on the shelf. I was explicitly instructed not to record or even perform for the rest of my contract, meaning I was legally bound not to do anything musical for three years.

Fortunately, I wasn't famous enough yet. I got another gig, and I kept my same name; no one from the record label found out.

I had a little money but needed to start building up my career again, so I started playing every night. But you can only do that for so long while neglecting your wife. She got lonely, and I didn't see it. But I realized soon enough that my marriage was in severe trouble when she found a guy and started a relationship with him behind my back. Or maybe I realized it when she brought that relationship out to the forefront. It was my fault, and it freaked me out, so I moved in with a buddy of mine in Orange County and started living down there.

That started things going downhill, and that was when I fully embraced living wild when the drugs got to be more and more of a mess-up. Then I met another woman, someone who was hot to trot and was moving to Hawaii.

So I thought, *Screw it, I'll just go to Hawaii with her.* I packed up what little I had and just moved out to Hawaii with her to lay on the beach and sing songs in Waikiki. We thought we had the Life of Riley living together, but the drugs were too much, and she started fooling around with almost all my friends.

What can I say? We were living wild. It was not a good life.

And it was during this time when I had a critical, life-changing experience while laying on the beach. I had spent the day surfing, smoking dope, and drinking beer with my buddy Harvey, and we were laying there talking about girls. At the time, it was pretty easy to get with someone—you just needed to buy them a lei of flowers and a few drinks, and that was it—and I was all in on that wild, carefree lifestyle. I thought I had it made, though I was going nowhere fast.

Harvey turned to me and said, "Which of these girls is the best you think you've ever had?"

"I guess they're all about the same," I said.

"So none of them comes to mind?"

And that was when I realized I was stuck on Colleen. "Well," I said, "there was this little Irish girl I met that I just think was the most beautiful thing that I'd ever laid eyes on in my life."

"So how was she in the sack?" Harvey asked.

"You know," I said, "I never touched her. Never even came close."

He couldn't believe me. "Really?" he said. "Then why would you think about her?" His question showed a lot of the mixed-up priorities we had; that a woman wasn't worth thinking about if you hadn't slept with her or had the opportunity to.

"I don't know, but I just can't get her out of my mind," I said in a moment of clarity. "She was just...just the most beautiful thing I'd ever laid my eyes on. She still is, I bet."

But before I could even think about being with Colleen, I needed to get my life back on track. And that was going to come about in a way I couldn't have anticipated.

CHAPTER 3

I need to tell you about my friend Jesse. She was a friend of mine who worked in the record business, and while I was in Hawaii, she would frequently call me or mail me little notes, just to check in with me. She wasn't a romantic interest—just a friend helping out another friend.

Anyway, in her notes, she'd always put in a little Scripture reference. She wouldn't write anything out, she would just put the chapter and verse, like "1 Corinthians 15:7," for example.

I hadn't brought much with me to Hawaii, but I did have an old Bible that my grandmother had given me, even though at the time I was the farthest possible distance from Christ or what anyone would consider a Christian. I mean, I was playing around with women, drugs, and booze, living the so-called "high life" in Waikiki. I thought I had it made, but by the same token, I was also so tired of giving myself away by sleeping around with all these women. I was ready for something different, and that's around the time Jesse started sending me these Scripture notes.

Every time I got a note, I would take down that old Bible and look up whatever Scripture Jesse sent, and inevitably I would think, *Wow! That kind of rings true.* I was kind of on a search for truth. I was tired of all the bull, and I wanted to know the truth.

Jesse had been working in the area of artist relationships at a couple of labels. She had an in at MCA Records, so she called me up one day.

"I've got you an audition for MCA Records if you're interested," she said. "But you have to come over here to the studio and record four songs, and then they'll look at you. If you're interested, I'll set it up."

"Yeah, sure!" I said. Though I was on a search for truth, I still longed for a recording career. So I sobered up a bit (I was still smoking my dope, but I thought I was pretty functional) and went over to the mainland, back to southern California.

I came over and stayed with a buddy of mine in Orange County and started reconnecting with people. Jesse and I got on the phone to catch up, and I asked her what she was doing.

"I was a ski instructor in Aspen," she said, "and my ex-husband called me and said he couldn't handle our kids anymore." She had three kids, and that was a surprise to hear that her kids were now living with her because back when I knew her before, she was not the kind of person you would think would be anything like a good mother. She was a drug-user, and a partier and her husband was a more conservative guy, and so ten years ago he'd split and taken the kids. Back then, we thought that was great because it gave her more time and less responsibility so she could party hard, but now here she was telling me that she was excited about being a mom.

And then she laid something on me:

"And I've become born-again Christian," she said.

"What?" I couldn't believe it! But now all those Scriptures made sense.

"Yeah, I became a born-again Christian."

Well, that was interesting! And unexpected.

"We're going to go into the studio on Monday," Jesse continued. "Why don't you come up and stay at my place? You know, sleep on the couch at my place. Just meet up with me at church on Sunday morning? That way you'll be fresh, and you won't have to fight the traffic coming up here to LA on Monday morning."

That sounded like a good idea, and accepting her hospitality was the least I could do since she lined me up for an audition. So I agreed.

Sunday morning came, and on the way up to the church, I hopped on the freeway in my buddy's old van. This van was a sixties love van, with a big mattress in the back (and yes, I'd spent a few times in that van). I was looking forward to rolling down the window and playing rock and roll music on the radio while driving on an LA freeway. I hadn't been back in about four years, and I thought it'd be kind of fun to sit up high listening to music and checking out all the chicks on the freeway.

There was nobody good-looking on the freeway that morning, and the speakers were blown in my buddy's van, making rock and roll impossible, so to pass the time I started meditating. I'd recently been dabbling in metaphysics—you know, Buddhism, reincarnation, stuff like that—and so I started meditating while driving (don't worry—I kept my eyes open), and I remember the conversation going something like this:

"God, Higher power...if Jesus is real, why don't you tell me about it? Or is he bunk? Is he real or is he bunk? I'd like to know."

I didn't get anything. I always felt some warm feeling when I meditated, but not that time.

So finally I said, "You know, I'm serious, I've read a lot of books, studied a lot of things, world religion and some of that. Just lay it on me, is He really real or is he bunk?"

Nothing.

In fact, it seemed like it was *more* than nothing. Like, black.

And then it was just dark. Not outside—I didn't see any actual darkness—but more like darkness, spiritually speaking. It was like I was not getting through to my higher power.

I kept driving, but it was like that for a bit until finally, I felt like I could "see" this little candlelight. And then I heard this little small voice:

"You don't want to know the truth," He said. "You just want me to confirm what you already believe."

"No, no!" I said. "I really want to know the truth, and I'm open to the truth."

Again the little candlelight and the little voice:

"You don't want to know the truth. You just want me to confirm what you already believe."

Well, that was the truth.

I thought God was going to say "Oh, you're so bitchin', you got this down, man, you've figured it out. You're just so wise and brilliant."

Could I handle the truth? The real truth and not what I was hoping to hear?

I didn't know, so I started praying a little more fervently about it, but it was black again. Finally, I thought to myself, *What if everything I believe is wrong? What if everything I put my life into and built my life on is a mistake? What would that be like?*

That scared me a little bit and so finally I came back, and I said: "You know, I've read a lot of stuff, I'm really smart, lay it on me."

And I hear this voice say, "You're nothing to me. You didn't create anything. I'm God. You're not God, I'm God. I don't owe you anything. Where were you when I formed the mountains and when I created the trees and all the animals? I don't owe you the truth."

Man, that scared me to death.

"God, I'll do anything if you tell me the truth," I said. "I'll give up women. I'll give up music. I'll give up drugs. I'll crawl on hot coals. I'll become a monk...just tell me the truth so I don't spend my life chasing after something fake."

I have no idea how I got to that point, but I did, and then I pulled into the parking lot of Jesse's church. I was crying big tears because I felt like I was going to waste my life here, and I got nothing, there's no light, no talking, no nothing, no small voice...just emptiness.

I pulled myself together and wiped away the tears and went

into the church. I found Jesse and her kids and sat down with them. The congregation was singing songs I'd never heard, love songs to Christ. I'd heard hymns and traditional songs like that, but I'd never heard a love song to Christ before. They sang "I Love You, Lord" and I remember thinking that I'd never heard anything so intimate in my life. I didn't believe in Jesus yet, but it was different. A right kind of different.

Then the pastor got up and started preaching this sermon on God's truth for man. So that felt like a weird coincidence, considering what I'd asked God on my way to church a few minutes earlier. At the end of the service, the pastor said, "If you want to know the truth about Jesus, raise your hand."

He didn't say, "If you want to give your heart to Jesus, raise your hand."

No, he just told us to raise our hands if we wanted to know the truth.

As I was sitting there, I heard the little small voice again:

"I thought you'd do anything to know the truth."

So I sheepishly raised my hand a little bit, no higher than my head.

Then the pastor said, "If you want to know the truth about Jesus, then stand up."

I wasn't about to stand up. I mean, I wasn't saying I believed in Jesus, I didn't want to do that, so I just sat still until I suddenly heard that small voice:

"You'll never see these people again. What do you care?"

So I slowly stood up.

Then the pastor said, "If you want to know the truth about

Jesus, then come down to the front of the church."

Well, I was raised Southern Baptist where, if you walked down to the front of the church, then the old ladies start kissing you, and dunked you by noon. I didn't want to do that. I mean, forget that, I didn't want to do that. So I started to sit down and all of a sudden, I heard the small voice say,

"This is your last chance if you want to know the truth. Do you really want to know the truth or not?"

I hightailed it down to the front of the church. But I still didn't believe it was Jesus.

I stood there and closed my eyes, and I didn't know what the pastor was saying because I was trying to meditate and think on God. You see, I thought he was gonna say, "Jesus is not it, it's something else." I don't know why I thought that, but that's what I thought.

When I was about five years old, I was with my grandparents on their ranch. Right down below their house, down the hill a little way, was a small cabin, another little house, where my great-grandmother lived, my grandfather's mother.

She used to wear long dresses, and one day her apron brushed the gas stove and caught on fire. So she came running up the trail screaming, aflame like a roman candle. The screaming caught our attention, and I jumped to the window only to see her running toward the house, burning and screaming. I just stared at the scene while my grandfather ran out the back door yelling, "Fall down! Fall down! Fall down!"

I remember her hair being on fire.

I remember my grandfather jumping on her, and right at the time he jumped on her it looked like his hand was on fire, his sleeve was on fire.

I remember my grandmother coming to me, grabbing my face, and shoving me into her apron as she guided me away from the window.

I tell you that story because as I stood there at the front of that church and listened to the pastor, I didn't—I couldn't—know what he was saying, I just had my eyes closed, and I felt a tingling from my toes all the way up my body.

It felt like I was on fire.

I remembered hearing my grandfather say, "Fall down! Fall down!"

And I stood there thinking, *God, burn me up, right here. Kill me right here. But I'm not moving 'til you tell me the truth.*

And then all of a sudden, I heard this voice:

"Your sins are forgiven. I died for you. You're white as snow."

I had not even said I believed, and He said He died for me. That my sins were forgiven. And all of a sudden, I saw all my sins, I saw my depravity of life and all the drugs and the sex, and I just felt terrible. I wanted to crawl into a hole and cover myself up, I was so ashamed to be in the presence of God and have all that filth in my life.

"No, Son, your sins are forgiven. You're white as snow."

I knew it was Jesus. I *knew* without a doubt it was Jesus.

And I just surrendered, I felt the old man inside of me die, and I knew in my heart of hearts that Jesus was real, that He died on the cross, rose from the dead, and that He did it because of my sin, which was ugly. I knew I was now different. I was washed clean and brand new.

Then they led us from the front of the church into a back room. Somebody wanted me to "speak in tongues." I had no clue what they were talking about but I found out they wanted me to blabber something, and I don't know why, but something came out of my mouth that I'd never heard before. I did a bunch of babbling, and I still didn't know what it was, and then I sort of stood there dumbfounded by the whole experience I'd just had.

But I knew it was true, and I was filled with joy.

I cried like a baby, just shocked.

They led me out the back door where I was reunited with Jesse and her kids; her daughter said she'd ride with me to show me the way to Jesse's house. So we went, and I had a million questions because her daughter was already a Christian. That poor little girl—I think she was about fourteen years old—I barraged her with all these questions, and then Jesse took me down to a Christian store and bought me a Bible. I became insatiable in the Bible, just reading day and night. And still to this day I'm insatiable. I love the Bible.

That night, I sat down with all those songs I was going to record the next day, and I changed all the lyrics. They were drug culture type songs, and I turned them into Christian songs. The next day I went to the studio and recorded, and they didn't like that at all. I kind of just blew the audition, but I didn't care. I mean, I knew the Lord of Lords, the King of Kings. I was just so excited I could hardly stand it.

I went back to Hawaii a Bible-loving, Christian pothead. I smoked my dope, and I read my Bible. I just kept smoking my dope and reading my Bible. After all, I was free!

I used to sell dope to tourists in the nightclub, especially since I found the Scripture that said that I'm free in Christ, and anything I want to do, I'm free in Christ. Of course, the next part says "Not everything you do is beneficial or profitable," but I kind of skipped over that part.

One morning I was cleaning my dope, smoking a joint, and the little Voice I heard on the LA freeway—which I now recognized as the Lord speaking to me—spoke up again:

"Do you like the way this stuff tastes?"

"No, I don't think it tastes good." I thought about it a second and said, "But I like how it makes me feel."

That was that, until the next day when I was doing the same thing, and God said:

"Do you like the way this makes you feel?"

Well, the feeling of being high wasn't like a rollercoaster ride or sex or anything like that, so I said, "No, not really."

God took me through about two or three days of those kinds of questions until finally, I realized I didn't like the taste or the feeling. In fact, everything about it was yuck.

Then one morning He said:

"What do they call this stuff?"

"Shit," I said. "We say we're smoking some good shit."

And God spoke to my heart:

"Well, where does that belong?"

I started laughing. "The toilet."

You can see where this is going. I took two and a half pounds of Maui red hair—that's fine marijuana—and I flushed it down the toilet.

And I never had a desire for it again.

About a week or so later, I was praying, and the Lord told me I was to come back to California, that this was where the trenches were and I was to get into the trenches and fight for the kingdom of God.

I didn't know what that meant, but I knew he was calling me, so I gathered my things and moved back to California and into my destiny.

CHAPTER 4

I hadn't seen Colleen for twelve years, and a lot had happened in that time. I should probably tell you a little bit about *her* childhood now, so that you can understand her better.

Colleen grew up in Saint George, Utah. Her grandpa was a rancher, and her mom and dad lived in Saint George. Like I said earlier, Colleen's dad was a truck driver, so he hauled long haul and was on the road for days on end.

He was not faithful to his wife—later on, we found out that he had a girl in almost every major city—so Colleen's parents ended up getting a divorce, which left her and her two sisters, high and dry in a Mormon town where divorce was frowned-upon and taboo. It was not good. Colleen's mom had a hard time with that.

Colleen's favorite memory was of her grandmother and grandfather, living life on the ranch, swimming in the water trough, and floating down what they called flood street on rainy days. She often spoke of those happy, childhood days when she and her two sisters, older sister Laura and younger sister Shelly, ran around with a single mom who had to work.

One year, Colleen's dad wanted to take the girls for the summer, but at the end of the summer, he decided not to let them go back home. So they stayed in California with their dad while their mom started up a new relationship and eventually got married to another guy.

For whatever reason, Colleen's mom didn't come after the girls, so Colleen was now in California, eleven years old, with a dad who didn't want her in the first place but just wanted to hurt her mom.

Her dad was not a good guy in a few ways. He had remarried, this time to a young wife who was like the wicked stepmother in Cinderella. She started by abusing the girls, pulling their hair, yelling and screaming at them. She worked them hard doing house-cleaning and laundry while she sat eating chips and watching TV. She did a lot more things that I won't go into here. Colleen didn't tell me all of it, but I knew enough about her to know it was terrible.

Probably the main things that showed the strength of my wife were her heart for justice and feisty temper. She was a bit stubborn, but I think she was perfect!

One day when Colleen was about sixteen, her stepmother came up from behind and pulled her hair. Colleen came up out of her chair and knocked the daylights out of her stepmom. The stepmom slid across the floor and hit the washing machine, and Colleen looked at her and said, "You will *never* touch me again, or I will kill you."

That scared the stepmom so much she never laid hands on Colleen again.

Colleen was miserable living there. She met a guy in high school who became her boyfriend, and he tried to talk her into fooling around, but she kept saying no, no, no, no...until finally he forced her into it and she said yes...and the first and only time she fooled around she got pregnant.

One time.

Her dad and stepmom kicked her out of the house and onto the street when they found out.

We didn't talk about it much, so I don't know exactly know how Colleen managed this part of her life. She used to walk two miles every day to take classes at her high school. Then she'd walk another mile to beauty school, then the three miles back home. All while pregnant.

When it came time to have the baby, rather than walking, she splurged and took the bus to the hospital. But she didn't have much money, and she definitely didn't have health insurance, so they wouldn't let her stay at the hospital beyond the bare minimum of one night. The next day she took her newborn angel and boarded another bus, where she met a young Hispanic woman who needed a home. Colleen being Colleen, she invited this young woman to live with her and help her take care of the baby. Colleen supported the baby, the young woman, and herself.

She also had to move a lot at first because her ex-boyfriend was a psycho who tried to kill her a couple of times; he even threw her down a flight of stairs while she was pregnant in an attempt to kill the baby. Fortunately, he finally gave up chasing her, and so she went on to raise her precious little girl.

Colleen was a tiny woman, only about 5 foot 1 inches tall, but she was the strongest person I'd ever met in my life, and she made up for her stature by having the biggest, most giving heart toward anyone in need.

When I got back from Hawaii, I started singing in a nightclub in Orange County just to make a living. One night, while I was performing, lo and behold Colleen's dad and stepmother came in. I didn't know any of the bad stuff about them at this point—just that they were customers and were nice to me. We started talking, catching up, and Colleen's dad mentioned something about his stepson, how messed up this kid was, on drugs and all kinds of stuff.

Having recently been a messed-up druggie myself, I just said, "The kid needs Jesus. That's the only thing that's going to get him out of it. He needs Jesus."

I know they thought I was crazy because that was different from who I'd been before.

Finally, at the end of the night, they said goodbye, and when Colleen's stepmom looked away, her dad wrote something in a matchbook and handed it to me. I stuck it in my vest, went back to my show, and completely forgot about it.

In those days, everyone smoked at the nightclub, so my clothes were utterly smoky, but I was so used to the smell that I didn't notice it. The next morning I went to Calvary Chapel in Costa Mesa, and as pastor Chuck Smith preached, all of a sudden I noticed I could smell stale smoke, and then I realized much to my embarrassment that it was *me*! I was wearing the same vest I'd worn the night before, and it was saturated. I couldn't get out of there quickly enough, so I went back to my apartment and decided to get it dry cleaned.

As I emptied the pockets before taking it to the dry cleaner, I found Colleen's dad's matchbook, and inside I saw a note in his handwriting:

"I want to know more about Jesus."

Well, at this point, I'd only been a Christian about a month, and I'd never had a chance to witness for Christ yet. So, man, I was excited. In Hawaii, all my friends would run from me when I would start talking about Jesus, but back in California, Colleen's dad wanted to know all about him.

I called him up, and I said, "Hey, can I come over?"

"Yeah, you can come over for lunch," he said.

So I went over for lunch, and when I walked into the house, there she was.

Colleen.

She was so beautiful. She was even more beautiful than before. I couldn't believe how beautiful she had become.

She had a little girl, Tasha, who was about eight, and she was beautiful, too, just absolutely adorable and fun. The kind of fun that you would tease with and play with. She was great.

I had some free tickets to a concert a buddy of mine was putting on. So I asked Colleen to go to the show with me, and she said no.

"C'mon," I said.

She still said no.

Finally, I appealed to her dad.

"You know," he said, "it would be a good thing if you'd go. What's the harm?"

We lined up the date; it was going to be in two weeks on Monday. We were going to go to this concert, but I got busy doing stuff, and I didn't call her for two weeks.

So I called her up that afternoon, Monday afternoon, and said, "I'll pick you up around 7:30."

"For what?"

"For our date," I said.

"You haven't called me in two weeks," she said. "I don't like flaky musicians. So, no, forget it, I'm not going out with you."

"C'mon, you promised."

"I can't find a babysitter at a moment's notice," she said. "I can't do that."

"You can't do that? What if I get your dad and stepmom to watch her?" I said.

"They're not going to."

"What if I could convince them? Would you go?"

She waited for a second. "Okay. If you can. Call me back."

I immediately called them and begged and begged, and they said they'd take care of her, so I got it all set up. That night I went over to Colleen's apartment; we dropped Tasha off with Colleen's folks and then headed to the concert.

We had the most wonderful time together. We talked and talked, and we didn't hold hands or anything. We just talked on the way to the concert, we talked after the concert, we talked all the way to a 24-hour coffee shop and then we talked until morning. I'd never met anyone more interesting in my life.

Her views on everything were terrific, her wit and her wisdom. I was just perplexed by how beautiful and smart she was. And we laughed so much! She thought I was crazy; I thought she was wonderful. It was the best night ever.

And then one night I asked her to go to Bible study with me. I had a Tuesday night Bible study at Calvary Chapel; she went with me a couple of times and afterward we talked about everything they'd taught.

So one afternoon we went out to get something to eat, and we went back to her house to sit and talk—we did a lot of talking; so much that we actually became best friends—and as we were talking, she said to me, "So how does a person become born again?"

She was raised Mormon, so she didn't have a clue about Christianity, nor did she know what I had been taught about the Bible. I didn't think she wanted to become born again—I thought she just wanted to know what it takes.

"You've got to know that you're a sinner," I said.

"Well, duh, we're all sinners," she said.

"Yeah, well, but, you have to believe that God loves you."

"Well, He made us, of course He loves us."

"Yeah, but you have to believe that He loves you so much that He became a man, Jesus," I said. "Jesus was His son, but they're like, one. So God like, becomes a man."

"Well, He's God, so God can do anything he wants to," she said. "So if God wants to become a man, He can."

"Yeah, yeah, that's right."

"Okay, He became a man, what else?"

"Well, He died for our sins," I said. "They killed God, they did that, they killed God. Hard to believe."

"Well, He's God, if He wanted to die, then He could die."

She was so smart.

"Yeah, well, that's true," I said.

"Well, what else?"

"Get this: three days later He rose from the dead."

"Well, Sam," she said, "He's God. He can die, He can raise from the dead, He can do anything He wants, He's God."

"Yeah, that's true, you're right."

"What else?" she said.

"According to this Scripture, it's Romans 10:9-10, it says if you believe that, and you accept Him as Lord in your heart, and you believe it, and you confess with your mouth, you'll be saved."

"So am I saved?"

"I don't know," I said.

"Well, I just confessed that I believe it, and I confessed it with my mouth, so am I born again, too?"

Remember how I had felt this tingling and burning and heard voices and all this other stuff? I thought *everyone* went through that when they gave their heart to Christ. They all heard these voices and bombs bursting in the air. But Colleen was a good girl, so it wasn't a big leap for her like it was for me. I was buried in the mire and the muck, and she had been a good, hardworking girl.

"Yeah, you're born again," I said.

"Well, I don't feel any different."

"According to this, you're born again. You're saved."

"Oh, good," she said, and that was that.

And so Colleen was the first person I ever led to Christ. And man did she get the real thing. I watched her blossom after that, and I watched her grow, and I watched her devour the word. She became insatiable in her Bible, and she had a million questions, and she took notes like crazy when we went to Bible study. She was just amazing.

Her wisdom was amazing, too. I remember one time we were having an argument and I brought out the old question of which came first, the chicken or the egg?

"Well, that's stupid," she said. "Everybody knows which came first."

"Okay, miss smarty-pants, what makes you so smart?"

"Everybody knows that the chicken came first."

"Really?" I said. "Philosophers have argued about that for hundreds of years. What makes you think you know?"

"It's simple," she said. "God would not make a baby and not give it a mother."

I don't know about you, but that's the smartest thing I've ever heard in my life. She looked at the character of God to learn about him. But that happened much later. At the time of this part of the story, I just liked Colleen, we were best friends, but there was no romance at all.

One night we went to a nightclub, and some guys started hitting on her, she was so beautiful, so she said to me, "Maybe we should just hold hands, so they'll know I'm with somebody."

I went, "Oh, okay."

So we held hands. And she had the softest hands; oh my gosh, her hands were soft.

Even though I was so heavy in like with Colleen, I thought

perhaps I should try to patch things up with my ex-wife, that maybe it was the godly thing to do. I wasn't dating, necessarily, except kind of with Colleen, but I thought, *Well maybe I'm supposed to make things right with my ex.*

So I called up my ex-wife, and I said I'd like to see her. I drove to LA where she lived and we went out, and grabbed a cup of coffee. She was living with a guy; it was not the guy she fooled around with before, it was another guy now.

And I told her about my newfound faith in God, but she just scoffed about God. It took me about two minutes with her to realize this was a mistake and that all I could think about was Colleen. I thought, *Wow, that's weird.*

We finished our coffee, I said goodbye to my ex-wife, and I haven't seen her since. That was over 34 years ago. And anyway I left, and all I could think about was getting back to Colleen.

Once I got home, I called Colleen and went over to her place where we talked and had a great time as always. She asked me about meeting with my ex, and I told her.

The next morning as I was praying, I prayed for Colleen and Tasha, something I had done every morning and night since we'd met again. I loved them, and I wanted them to do well. I thought, *Lord, Colleen needs a godly man in her life. She's such a good girl; she needs a godly man in her life.* So I prayed for her to find a godly man.

And then after I finished praying for her, I decided to pray for myself. So I was praying, and I thought, *You know God, I've been celibate, and I'm trying to stay that way, and I don't mind being a monk if that's what you want, just be a celibate guy and serve you. But you know, I kind of wish I could share my life with somebody, and I would kind of*

*like to have something healthy and strong, a godly girl. So could you give
me a godly girl?*

And I felt as though the Lord spoke to my heart and He said:

"She's right in front of your face."

"Who?"

"Colleen. Who else?"

"Colleen?"

"She's the one I had planned for you from the beginning."

I was so excited! I mean, she was everything I've ever wanted.
She was gorgeous and smart and hardworking, and she was just
absolutely perfect.

So I called her on the phone, and I guess this sounds like I'm
not the brightest bulb in the package—it seems stupid—but I called her
and I said, "Colleen, guess what? Guess what? I'm getting married!"

"What?" she said.

"Yeah, I'm getting married!"

She started crying! I could tell on the phone, just her little
tears, before she finally said, "To who?"

"Well, to you!" I said. "Who else?"

"What are you talking about?"

I said, "I was praying, and God told me that I'm supposed to
marry you. God told me that. That it was supposed to be you."

And she started crying even more.

"What's wrong?" I asked.

"I was praying, and I felt as though God said I was supposed to
marry you," she said. "But I wasn't sure if that was Him. I thought it
was maybe just my desire."

"No, Honey, no. It's the truth. You and I are supposed to be
one."

Then she got very Colleen: "Sam Parsons," she said, "you can't do this over the phone. You need to do this in person."

"Okay!" So I hung up the phone and drove over to her house.

I remember her opening the door, and me just looking at her and her looking at me. We had never hugged before or anything, and I wrapped my arms around her.

It was like a hand in a glove.

It was a perfect fit.

We just held each other, and we both cried.

And we praised God.

Finally, I said, "So, will you marry me?"

"Of course I will! God wants us to be married."

"Yeah."

We dated some more, planning the whole time on getting married, until finally one day I said, "You know what? Let's go get our license, to prepare for when we're ready."

I was already on my lunch hour, so we went down to the courthouse to get the license, and while we were standing there in the line, there was this little couple next to us who got married at the next window over. The Justice of the Peace married them right there!

I thought, *Man, I could save five thousand bucks right here if I could talk her into it.*

"You know you love me," I said.

"Yeah."

"You know I love you."

"I do."

"I don't know about you, but I don't want to wait," I said. "I want us to get married soon."

"Yeah, I know."

Before she knew it, I had guided us over to that line where the couple has just gotten married. And so finally I said, "Why don't we just get married right now?"

And before she could say anything we were standing up at the window. A Justice of the Peace came up, and we'd just bought our license; he took it and married us right then and there.

We didn't even know what hit us. We were both dumbfounded.

Then I went back to work because I didn't tell my boss I was going to get married, I was just going to get a license. So I had to go back to work while Colleen went back to the place where she was living. I said I'd see her after work, and we met up later that night.

I never lived it down. Every time we went to a wedding after that, she'd get mad at me because I was performing other people's weddings while we didn't have one.

But that's how we started our life together, just two kids who were just fresh in love with the Lord and fresh in love with each other.

CHAPTER 5

When it came to being married, Colleen and I didn't know what we were doing, but fortunately, we had some good influences in our lives. One was an older couple who had been married sixty years. Fred and Virginia were mentors to us, and as a couple, we watched them and just thought, *Man, we want to be like them.* We modeled our lives on being lovey like them; we loved that.

Fred got sick, and I went to sing for him and pray for him; later Colleen and I went to pray over him together. I think he died of the same thing I have, pancreatic cancer. At any rate, when we did Fred's funeral, we opened up a time for people to share.

One guy stood up, and he raised his hand, and said, "Fred saved my marriage."

So of course, with that, we all listened intently.

The man said, "My wife and I were on the verge of divorce, ready to file papers, and I went to Fred and said 'Fred, I don't get it, you and Virginia seem so much in love, how can you do it? What's your secret to making a marriage work? I've tried and I've tried, it's not working.'"

And Fred told him, "Virginia and I have two secrets. First of all, we always put God first. Whenever we make a decision, we pray about it, and God never tells Virginia something different than He tells me. It's always the same, and we don't make a move until we know that we both agree that it's the Lord telling us. That's the first secret.

"The second secret is: I have made it my life's ambition every day try to find six new ways every day to show Virginia that I love her. I've been so busy trying to find new ways to show her that I love her that I haven't had time to find any of her faults yet."

That so took me. I went home, and Colleen and I sat down and talked, and I said, "Honey, I want us to live by these two rules. I want us always to seek God first, and we don't decide until we know it's God."

"I like that," she said. "Let's do that. Let's commit ourselves to that."

"And I want it to be my life's ambition to try to find new ways to tell you how much I love you every day."

"I like that, too. Let's do that."

So we've spent our entire lives living that way, making decisions and showing each other how much we love each other.

One of the first decisions Colleen and I made together happened when we were brand-new Christians. She came to me one day and she said, "What do you think about tithing?"

We'd just heard a sermon on it at church, and I said, "I don't know. I feel like we should, but how can we? We're broke."

We were barely scraping by as it is, I mean I saved pennies to buy gas. It was pretty bad.

"I don't know," she said, "but I think we should." She was such a giver.

"How would we do that?"

"I think we should commit to three months of tithing on everything we get, and let's see if the windows of heaven open up at the end of three months."

So we committed ourselves to it, we prayed about it—we prayed about everything—and we started tithing; we tithed and tithed, and every week we tithed. On any nickel and dime that came in, we tithed.

After three months we looked at it, and the windows of heaven still seemed pretty closed.

"I know the windows of heaven haven't opened up," Colleen said, "but you know, honey, we're not any worse off than before."

Okay, at least we were obedient. "Yeah, I guess that's true," I said.

"Let's just keep doing it until God tells us not to."

We never stopped.

We've tithed on every penny we ever made from that point forward.

Years later I ran into a guy who was at our first church when we started tithing, and he said, "You know the thing I remember, Sam? How much you and Colleen blessed us."

"How did we bless you?"

"Well, I was the treasurer of the church, and I knew what everybody gave. Every week, you would give $11.22, or $25.18. Right down to the penny of tithing, just every week it was to the penny."

I didn't know what to say.

"I watched that for years," he continued, "and I would marvel that people that had a lot of money weren't giving but you guys were giving every penny."

I want to take credit for that, but in truth it was Colleen.

I remember one time we were at a 7-11 getting a Diet Coke, and I came out, and a homeless guy was asking for money. I got in the car, and Colleen goes, "You need to give him twenty bucks."

"You don't know if that guy's going to buy drugs or booze," I said. "We don't know this guy; I don't want to give him twenty bucks."

"Honey, you give him the money," she said. "This guy needs this money more than we do. Let God decide what he'll do with it. But you give it in Jesus name, and you pray for him."

So I got out of the car, but by the time I finished arguing about it, he was gone. I was not sad about that. "Honey, he's gone, he's not there."

"I think he walked down this way," she said. "Let's go down that way." So we started driving down the street until we saw some guys in an alley.

"Go down there and see if you find him," she said.

"I could get mugged in that alley!"

"God is with you, don't worry about it. You give that guy twenty bucks, and you tell him it's in Jesus's name. And you pray for him."

And you know what? I did. I walked down the alley, and sure enough, there he was, and so I gave him the twenty bucks and said: "This I give to you in Jesus name, I want to pray for you."

I don't know what happened to that man, but I know that I obeyed.

Colleen always made me ten times a better man than I was.

Probably one of the most significant points of my life happened because of Colleen. She was praying for my dad, even though he and I had a terrible relationship. My dad loved Colleen and thought she was just the greatest thing in the world.

My mother, though, didn't feel the same; she had this jealousy thing, and I don't know what that was about. You know, I had the most wonderful mother; she was just great when I was a boy. She would cook things, and laugh around the house, and sing, and she was just the sweetest thing. I adored my mom, and I thought she was going to adore Colleen, but when we got married, Colleen and Mom just didn't hit it off. It was Mom, not Colleen. Colleen tried.

Colleen was loving and kind to my mom, but my mom turned into kind of a battleax of a mother-in-law. She treated Colleen terribly, though I didn't notice it at first.

Then Colleen finally said to me one day, "Your mom doesn't like me."

"What do you mean? Who would not like you?"

"She doesn't like me."

"My mom loves everybody!"

"Well, she doesn't like *me*," she said. "I don't know why. I've tried and tried and tried to be sweet to her, but she treats me terribly."

"Oh, Honey, you're exaggerating."

Colleen wanted so much to have a good mom relationship, but it just wasn't happening with my mother.

Anyway, one time my mom came down to stay with us for a few days. One evening I was sitting at the piano in our little music room off to the side of the kitchen. I wasn't playing; I was writing something, using the piano as a sort of desk, so I was quiet and, since the piano wasn't visible from the kitchen, I was also out of sight.

Mom was at the stove. I was raised on beans and cornbread, and so she was making beans with ground beef in it and homemade cornbread. I know most people think that sounds stupid, but to me, it was the greatest meal in the world.

Colleen came into the kitchen just as sweet as could be, and I heard her say, "Hi, Mom, what are you making? It smells so good."

Mom said, "I'm making beans and cornbread, but not enough for you!"

Colleen was just devastated. That remark just cut her to the quick, and so she came out of the room with tears in her eyes. She looked at me and said, "I told you. I don't know why she doesn't like me. I told you."

Then she walked out of the room, still crying.

That led to one of the hardest conversations I've ever had. I had to sit down with my mom and say, "Mom, I love you with all my heart, but you are never to talk to my wife like that again. She's my wife, we're one, and if you love me, you have to love her. And if you can't treat my wife nicely..."

My mom started objecting. "Honey, I don't know what you're

talking about."

"Mom, I was right behind the door here, and I heard you snap at her."

"Oh, I didn't snap at her."

"Oh, yes, you did. And I don't know why. She's trying to be sweet to you, and you're treating her terribly. Mom, I love you, and you're welcome in my house but not if you talk to my wife like this. We won't have anything to do with you. Because my wife comes first."

It was a hard conversation and a hard next few days. Mom was hurt, and I was hurt, and Colleen was totally hurt until finally my mom went back home and things seemed to get a little better.

Over the years it was sad, I remember at my mom's funeral, everyone talked about how nice my mom was, and Colleen just cried the whole service. When we got out of the funeral, which I'd conducted, and we got back to our hotel room, Colleen was sobbing.

"What's wrong?" I asked.

"Your mom never let me see that side of her," she said. "Everybody said how sweet and loving she was, but she never showed me that. I feel like I missed so much. Am I so hard to love that a mom can't love me?"

I put my arm around her. "Honey, what's going on?"

"What's wrong with me?" she said "That a mother can't love me? What's wrong with me?"

God, it broke my heart. Because she was the most loving person you could ever know.

I started this chapter by saying how much my dad loved Colleen. She may not have had my mother's heart, but my dad thought she was the cutest thing in the world and she loved him right back.

Whenever my parents would come down, she just spoiled him rotten, whatever his favorite thing was, she would cook for him. She just loved my dad, and he was so sweet to her; maybe that's why my mom was jealous, I don't know.

Me? I had this thing with my dad. My dad was heavy-handed with me as a boy. And because of that, well, I hate to say it, but I hated my dad.

He was sweet to Colleen but cold to me; I'd never heard the words, "I love you" from my dad. I didn't understand that. Maybe he said it when I was little, but I don't remember hearing him say that. So we had this bad rub of a relationship, and I never felt like I measured up.

One night I was out mowing the lawn at 9:30 because my dad was coming the next day. It was pitch dark outside, so Colleen came out and said, "What are you doing?"

"I'm mowing the lawn," I said. "I want the yard to look good for my dad."

"Honey, you can't see what you're doing."

I was mowing it over and over again so I wouldn't miss any spots. And she walked back in the house, and I remember just sitting on the grass crying thinking, *Man, you're a sick puppy. You have to try and please your dad, and you're never going to satisfy your dad.*

It was sad.

Colleen came to me one day and said, "Honey, I've been praying about your dad."

"Yeah?"

"I bought you a ticket to go see him."

"Honey, that's the money we were saving for our couch."

"We can get a couch later, but you need to go see your dad," she said. "I feel it's important. You need to iron all this stuff out with him."

Well, you know, coincidentally I had been praying about my relationship with my dad for a long time, and I'd finally got to a point where I was reading the Ten Commandments, and it said, "Honor thy father and mother," and every time I'd think about it, it'd turn me off because I didn't want to honor my dad. I didn't like him!

I remember talking to the Lord one time and saying, "You know Lord, I don't know how I can honor him for all the beatings, the emotional abuse, and all the bad stuff. That he would call me lazy so much that I turned into a workaholic to prove him wrong."

And the Lord said:

"My law is always higher than your justification."

"But, Lord, I'm justified in hating this guy."

And the Lord said again:

"My law is always higher than your justification. No matter what you feel justified in, My law is higher. You're to honor your father."

"How do I honor him?" I asked.

"Is there anything good in your dad?"

At that time, I didn't think there was. Except for maybe one thing: he was the hardest-working man I'd ever met.

So the Lord said:

"From now on when you talk about your dad, you just say 'He's the hardest-working man I've ever met.'"

So I did. And then I thought about how my dad was great to my mom. He loved my mom; he adored my mom. He showed me how to love a woman. My dad completely loved my mom, and he treated her like a queen. So I added that to what I'd say about him. "He's a hard worker, and he treated my mom good. He showed me how to love a woman; that's a good thing, I guess."

Not long after that, I said to the Lord, "I'm not ready to forgive my dad, but I've realized that I need to. If you would make me willing to be willing that I could forgive my dad, I would. I'm not willing. You have to make me willing."

Colleen kept praying for me because I hurt so much from it until I finally came to a point where I really understood that my dad didn't know the Lord, so why would I expect him to walk in a godly way when he didn't know the Lord? And so I prayed and prayed hard for months and then one day:

I realized I had forgiven my dad.

Not only did I forgive him, but I started to fall in love with him.

Any time I called my parents' house, my dad would answer the phone, and I would say, "Hey, Dad, it's me."

Then he would always say, "Here's your mom," and hand off the phone.

Every time it happened like that.

Until one time I said, "Dad, it's me. I love you."

He hesitated before saying, "Here's Mom."

Another day I made another phone call, and I said, "Hey, Dad, I love you." And there was a silence on the phone, and he said "Okay. Here's your mother."

Then another day I said, "Dad, I love you."

And there was silence.

And he goes, "Me too. Here's Mom. "

I flew on Cloud Nine for two weeks over that "Me too."

And then finally I said "I love you," and my dad said, "I love you too, son."

And then he kept talking.

After a minute, I said, "Well, you probably ought to let me talk to Mom."

"No, you talk to me this time. You can talk to Mom next time."

We had a great conversation, and I don't even remember what it was about! But I do remember that, before we hung up, he said, "I love you, son."

Wow! I mean, I cried like a baby for a week!

It was not long after that experience and the forgiveness of my dad that Colleen brought me the tickets and told me to see him. I'd forgiven him, but I was nervous to see him in person. But I still went to see my dad, and I spent five days with my folks. I think they thought Billy Graham came for a visit because I preached at them all five days.

Soon enough, Sunday morning came. I was scheduled to fly back home that afternoon, so I woke up and packed and got dressed for church, then came out to find my mom and dad both dressed in Sunday go-to-meeting clothes.

"What are you guys up to?" I said.

"We decided we want to go to church with you," my dad said.

"Really?"

"Yeah."

"Great!"

So we went to church, and I sat by my parents while the preacher preached a salvation message.

It got near the end of the service and the music started, and the guy did what we call an altar call, asking if anybody wanted to give their heart to Christ.

Suddenly I heard my dad sniffling a bit; I looked over, and I'd never seen him like that before: he was crying.

"Dad, are you alright?"

"No."

"What's wrong?"

"I've got to give my heart to Jesus," he said.

He was petrified, stuck in the pew.

"Dad, if I walk down the aisle with you, would you walk down the aisle with me?"

"You'd do that?"

"Yes, sir!"

"Alright," he said, "if you walk down there, I'll go with you."

So my dad and I locked arms, and we walked down the aisle so my dad could give his heart to Jesus. And it felt like the most exciting thing in my life.

I would have never gone to visit him had it not been for the wisdom of my wife.

Mine and Colleen's relationship was built on trust—especially trusting in God. Some years ago, we hit a brick wall, financially. I was out of work, and we were down to only 8 cents, and that we had scrounged out of one of the kid's piggy banks.

I had been working for a Christian radio station and, long story short, I ended up out of work. I'd also been playing nightclubs, for quite a while, to help make ends meet, and Colleen was in the middle of a high-risk pregnancy, so she couldn't work. Just before losing my job at the Christian radio station, I had decided to quit singing in nightclubs; I was going to dedicate my music to God wholly. Wouldn't you know it?! The timing was perfect; I left the nightclub job, then the Christian radio station job ended and immediately my commitment was tested.

Was I going to trust God, as it said in Matthew 6:33: "Seek first His kingdom and His righteousness and all these things you need will be added," or was I going to cave in and go out and stir up another nightclub gig? But I had made a commitment to dedicate my music to God. I was stuck.

Did I trust God or not?

I was reading my Bible early one morning, studying the story of Abraham and Sarah. I reached the part where Sarah gave her maidservant, Hagar, to Abraham to help God out a bit with His promise of a child. In other words, they were taking matters into their own hands to receive God's blessing of their promised child. As I read on, I watched the mess unfold, and it hit me: "If I go out and start singing my songs for the devil, just to feed my children, (and I could easily find a job doing that) it would probably end up costing us in the end."

Now, I was raised to be a hard worker; I don't like laziness. My dad instilled in me a strong work ethic—remember that was the one good thing I could say about him back when I needed to forgive him. But it was hard to sit back and wait for God to move. So...I didn't. I went out looking for work every day. But nothing came of it.

Finally, Colleen in her wonderful, Godly kind of wisdom said, "Let's just pray for a day or so, and let God tell us what to do." So, we did. We fasted for three days searching for an answer.

Our rent was coming due, and we were hard-pressed. Some months earlier, I had done a lot of voiceover work for someone on some radio advertising, but they had failed to pay me. Out of the blue one afternoon, they sent us a check. Our rent got paid.

We were almost out of food. Then one morning, just after

praying together, I heard a knock on our front door but, when I went to answer it, there was no one there—instead I found a box of food on our front doorstep. We ate.

After days of prayer, I felt an urge to buy a newspaper and look for a job.

"Where did the urge come from?" Colleen asked

"I think it was put there by the Lord," I said.

"Thank you, Lord!"

That day I found work. We were learning to build our house, our home, our spiritual foundation on the Rock. God was working in our hearts.

It was, and still is, a hard learning process. There have been many times when friends of ours have said to us, "Boy I wish we had your faith." In all honesty, we have no other choice. We have seen Him work in our lives, and we have seen the frustration that comes from not trusting Him. It's a no-brainer.

In John 6, just after Jesus introduces the concept of communion for the first time, many of his disciples didn't want to hear it. They couldn't understand it. So they left.

Yet Peter stayed behind. Jesus asked him why he wasn't leaving, too, and in verses 68 and 69, Peter gives the reason: "Lord to whom shall we go? You have words of eternal life, And we have believed and have come to know that You are the Holy One of God."

Do you think it is easy to have the kind of faith Peter had? I mean, Peter had walked with God and talked with God. He had observed the feeding of the 5000; he had watched Christ heal the blind, the deaf, the lame, and the sick. Peter had even walked on water with Jesus and had been with Jesus on the Mount of Transfiguration where he'd seen Moses and Elijah and heard the voice of God.

Perhaps if we walked with God and talked with God and observed the miracles around us as Peter did, it might be easier. But easy? No, I don't think so. I don't think God wants it to be easy. If there is a key here, it has to be wrapped up in a real intimacy with Christ, daily walking and talking, reliance on Him.

The children of Israel saw the Red Sea split, ate the manna from heaven, followed the pillar of fire, and the cloud of God's glory. They received promises that were so wonderful that it is almost impossible to believe they would ever stray. But they did, over and over again.

I think true faith, a true foundation built on the Rock is only when we truly know Jesus, intimately! It is not just what you know, but who you know. **Without faith, there is no intimacy.** This is true with any relationship, but especially true in regards to our relationship with God.

I needed that faith, that trust, because I was about to go through it again with my dad.

About a month after my dad had given his heart to Christ we got a phone call, and he delivered some long-overdue news. We knew he'd been a little sick, he said he needed to tell me something.

He had stage-four colon cancer.

I went up to visit him a couple of times, and even though my mom was not too friendly, Colleen still loved my dad, and she wanted to come up and see him also. So we took the kids and drove to see him.

As I was sitting with my dad, talking to him about life and regrets, I asked him, "Dad, how are you doing with this dying thing?"

"Well, I've never been in such a powerful position," he said.

It's funny because I didn't get it at the time, but now I'm in that same position, I know exactly how he felt.

"If I live, that'll be a miracle of God, and that means he has work for me," he said. "And if I die, I get to go to heaven. I've never been in such a powerful position."

Then he looked at me and gave a smile, and here he was, lying in bed, weighing about a hundred pounds, and he said, "Son, you know what? You beware of a man who's got nothing to lose. I'm a dangerous individual."

And he laughed.

He called me on Father's Day, a few months before he died.

"Hey, I'm supposed to call you," I said.

"Ah, it won't hurt this time."

We talked for a few minutes, and then he said, "I called to apologize."

"Dad, what do you need to apologize for, what'd you do? I've already forgiven you for everything, what are you apologizing for?"

"I hit you too hard, and I hit you too often, and I'm really sorry."

It felt like I had these little hairline cracks in my heart I didn't even know were there, and when he said that, they just healed up.

You know the strangest miracle of all is that I used to hate my dad, and then I fell in love with him. And because I chose to forgive my dad for all those things, I don't have any wounds of that little boy anymore. God's healed my heart completely, and now I just love my dad.

I'll see you soon, Dad.

CHAPTER 6

Probably one of the hardest lessons about prayer and learning to trust God came when Colleen and I were told we might lose our son, Nick. Nick was diagnosed with terminal leukemia when he was only 2½ years old, and the events at that time almost unraveled our lives; it was indeed our eleventh hour. It brought us to the end of our rope and face to face with God.

I was working as a sales manager for a national sign company. The job was a good job, but it took a lot of hours, and the pressure of all the deadlines was unbelievable. From early morning till late night, I was fighting with one person or another. There were disputes about construction delays, under-pricing, over-pricing, inferior materials, miscommunications, lying, and cheating. I had a boss who had 40,000 ulcers and intentions on passing a few of those ulcers over to me. At the same time our family was growing, and although it was an exciting time, it was also very hectic.

Colleen and I already had three kids and another one on the way. At the time of this story, Natasha was about 12, Nick was 2½, and Alyssa was only about six months old. Colleen was beautifully pregnant, and I was a very proud husband and father. Everything looked like we had it made. Then all at once, our world started falling apart.

It started with Nick. He was always a very busy, energetic boy. If you look in the dictionary under the word *active*, you would find Nick's picture. He put a whole new meaning to the phrase "Terrible Twos." One morning, Nick started to complain about his little tummy, and by afternoon he was white as a ghost and lethargic.

The next day we took him to our family doctor, who looked him over and said he probably had the flu. We put Nick to bed, but Colleen didn't feel right about it. We continued to monitor him for the next few days, but instead of getting better, he just seemed to get worse and worse. He never threw up or did anything else that looked like the flu; he just lay still, looking pale and lethargic. We were genuinely beginning to worry.

We went to the doctor's office once again and asked them

to run some blood tests. They acted like we were just over-excited, nervous parents, but they agreed to run tests anyway.

Nick's condition continued to worsen over the next couple of weeks. After quite a few tests, the doctor called us in one afternoon and said, "We've found something, but we don't want to venture a guess until we've run some further tests."

Of course, we agreed, and the more tests began. Blood tests, X-rays, physical exams, more blood tests, more doctors got involved.

And then the news came.

I'll never forget that day.

I was driving down the freeway, on my way to a sign installation, when I had this feeling I should call the doctor's office. We didn't have cell phones in those days, so I pulled over to a phone booth in front of a 7-Eleven and called. When the doctor came on the line, he asked me to come in and see him right away. I knew the news was going to be bad by the tone of his voice.

"I am a man of faith, and I can handle it," I said, "but I need to know right now."

He hesitated for a second then said, "Mr. Parsons, your son has leukemia, and we believe it may be terminal."

I stood there in shock, stunned, numb and out of breath. I don't know how, but I thanked him and asked that he not call my wife. "I will tell her," I said. "I will call you later, doctor." Then I hung up the phone.

I stood there staring at all the traffic zooming by, thinking to myself, *No one knows that my world is exploding around me.* I adore my son; he is the apple of my eye.

I climbed into my truck, feeling like a semi had hit me. I somehow got back on the freeway, driving to God only knows where, and I began to cry uncontrollably. I was sobbing, crying out, "Please Lord, don't take my boy!, I love him so much, Father. Please Lord, oh God, NO! NO! NO! Daddy, Daddy, oh Daddy, what am I going to do?"

I remember weeping and wondering to myself, *Which Daddy am I crying to?* I just kept crying, "Daddy, Daddy, Daddy." I was crying so hard I could no longer see the road and had to pull over. I somehow gained enough composure, after quite a while of sobbing, to hurriedly head straight home.

I tried to be as gentle as I could when I broke the news to Colleen, but she began to sob as well. We held each other and cried together for quite awhile.

Then we dropped to our knees and began to pray to God for help.

The next morning we went straight to the doctor's office and asked for a second opinion. He brought in two specialists who confirmed the prognosis. We asked to see a hematologist, a cancer doctor, anyone for another opinion. The doctors started to get upset with us for doubting them. One of the doctors even pulled out a booklet on how to handle baby death, and I was furious! They told us we were overreacting, that we needed to resolve ourselves to the facts and settle down.

I wanted to hit someone, but I restrained myself. We left upset and still sobbing, but we were resolved to find a doctor who could offer us some hope, one who might believe in God.

Nick continued to get weaker and started having trouble with his little tummy, and he was still pale as a ghost. It broke our hearts to see him just laying on the couch, without even enough energy to raise his little head. By now we had been to two other hospitals and met with three hematologists who had given Nick MRIs, CAT scans, blood tests, X-rays; you name it, we tried it. It's almost a blur to me now, yet it is burned into my memory all at the same time.

Because of Nick's upset stomach symptoms and abdominal pain, we decided to search out a doctor who worked with intestines and stomachs—internal stuff. I know that doesn't sound very technical, but all we knew to do was stay focused on Nick, and try to find someone to help us. We were grasping at straws, and we were not going to leave one stone unturned.

The doctor we found, who specialized in gastric disorders, was very well respected at Children's Hospital in Orange. His bedside manner was terrible, but boy, was he thorough. He took over.

He admitted Nick into CHOC Hospital (Children's Hospital of Orange County) and put together a team of specialists. Colleen and I finally felt like someone was hearing us. We had a new ray of hope.

One week before going to CHOC, I had been searching the Scriptures for an answer, some hope, some direction. I found a Scripture in the book of James that brought me hope.

"Is any of you sick? He should call the Elders of the church to pray over him and anoint him with oil in the name of the Lord. And the prayer offered in faith will make the sick person well; the Lord will raise him up." (James 5:14)

I read it over and over again, I prayed and prayed about it, and then I called the head Elder of our church and made the request for them to come. The head elder was a very nice brother. He said they had been praying for us. But when I told him what I had read in James 5, that we were to "call the Elders of the church to pray," he sounded unsure.

He said, "We don't normally do that sort of thing, anointing with oil."

I told him we sincerely wanted them to come.

"I don't even know what kind of oil to use," he said.

"I don't care if you use 30-weight motor oil, it's not the oil that heals him, it's the Lord," I said. "We have to have faith and follow what He tells us to do. Isn't that right?"

I had tried to explain to Nick what was about to happen, that it was going to be kind of fun and exciting. He wasn't yet three years old and couldn't quite grasp it, but I didn't want him to be any more scared than he already was. Faithfully, our Elders showed up at the house, olive oil in hand, and humbly submitted to God's Word. They anointed little Nick. We all prayed and cried together. It was a great moment in our family history. We felt strengthened and encouraged.

Now, two weeks later, we were in Children's Hospital with a team of specialists, poking Nick for blood samples every 30 minutes. Nick kept crying, "Daddy don't let them poke me, Daddy! Please, Daddy, help me!" I felt so helpless, and afraid and I felt like such a mean dad for letting them poke him so much. But what was I to do? Colleen was there as much as she could be, but with two other kids and her being pregnant, it was an impossible situation. They wouldn't let her go into the rooms where they performed the CAT scans or X-rays, and someone had to stay home to care for the other kids. What a mess we were in!

And I haven't even mentioned my job situation during all this mess...

When I told the owner of my company what was going on, she was wonderful about it. She said, "Take all the time you need, we are behind you." I was in charge of sales territories at the time. I had a good team of salespeople, but I was the one in charge and I had to make it all work. I had the responsibility of overseeing every aspect of the sign sale, from sales management and construction to delivery and installation, and even making sure the bills got paid. This meant city permits and customer complaints, as well as salespeople complaints, and, of course, management pressures.

As the week wore on, there in the hospital, I began to receive call after call from my boss. What about this? What about that? Who does this? Who does that? When are you coming back? This problem, that problem, on and on and on; the issues were getting out of control, and I was being pulled apart.

I was already overwhelmed with taking care of Nick, not wanting to miss a moment with him. I wanted to know everything about his condition and his care. I couldn't leave him for a second—I hated to leave him alone even to go to the bathroom.

One morning, as the doctors performed a spinal tap on him, I was holding Nick's hand concentrating on being encouraging, when a phone call came directly into the operating room. It was my sweet, supportive boss suddenly demanding I drop everything and get my rear end immediately into the office or I would be out of a job! I was so upset and frustrated, and it took all my strength not to give her a good, old-fashioned "sailor type" cussin'.

I, in all honesty, yet ashamedly, must admit I did tell her where she could stick her job, and her company.

"I am in the middle of something here a bit more important than you and your stupid little sign company," I said.

I realize that was not the smartest thing to say to your boss, but I was tired, I was scared about my boy, and I had not had a good night's sleep in almost two weeks.

We got Nick out of CHOC on a Wednesday afternoon, just three weeks before Christmas. There was still no change in Nick's prognosis, but then again, his new test results were not back yet.

When Nick and I arrived home, we found his mom crying and all upset. I thought it was her distress over Nick, but it was another bit of bad news. Colleen proceeded to tell me that she'd had a visitor that morning, a U.S. Marshal, who had come to our door to deliver a Notice of Eviction. We had been renting the home we were in for only about six months, and we had never been late on the rent. However, our owner/landlord could not say the same about making his mortgage payments on time. It seemed he had an Owner Occupied Home Loan, which meant he was supposed to be living on the property. BUT! He had not been making his house payment for over six months. Thus he, as the occupant—meaning us—was being evicted. We had to vacate, be off the property by January first. Shock City! What else could go wrong?

(By the way, I've learned never to ask that question.)

The next morning I went into the office to apologize to my boss for my overreaction to her phone call.

It was a very chilly meeting.

She informed me that she was distraught by my lack of caring about my job and the company and that she was demoting me to sales representative and giving me a new territory. Now I don't know if you know very much about commission sales, but while a territory commission sales job can bring in a healthy income, that only happens after you have built up your territory accounts, and it can take months to do that.

My boss also informed me that she was not going to pay my salary for the previous two weeks, since I'd spent most of my time at the hospital and the company had lost money; she was sorry, but that's the way it goes.

No salary, no income. In other words, I was, for all intents and purposes, out of work. "Thank you very much, do not go pass go, do not collect *any* dollars. Bye-bye!"

I was stunned, angry, and speechless. Three weeks till Christmas, no money, no job, a dying boy, and we had to be moved out by January first. Could it get any worse, or more overwhelming?

Don't ask, because...yes, it can!

I woke up early one morning, which wasn't hard to do since I wasn't able to sleep anyway. I drove down to the nearest liquor store where they drop the morning papers for the paper boys, and I waited to get the first paper. I grabbed it, ran home, and highlighted every sales job I thought I had a shot at. I showered, got dressed in my finest get-a-new-job suit, and hit the trail before the sun was up.

I was hard at it for the best part of the day, when suddenly my pager went off. It was a beep from home. I kind of panicked; I thought it was probably about Nicky. I hurriedly pulled over to the first phone booth I could find. It was out of order, so I rushed to another; it was out of order, too. I ran across the street to another one that was working and quickly phoned home. Tasha, our 12-year-old daughter, answered the phone.

"It's the baby, Daddy, it's the baby!" she cried. "Momma rushed to the hospital! It's the baby, Daddy! "

"It's okay, Honey, Daddy is on his way! Just sit tight, I'll be there as soon as I can. Everything is going to be alright."

I jumped in my little truck and hit the road, driving like a madman. I even drove down the side of the road when someone got in my way. I hit 100 miles an hour a few times, I also topped the speedometer and pinned it for a few minutes. I was scared to death that Colleen and I were losing our baby. Colleen had been under such tremendous stress, and this pregnancy was a hard one. I barreled into the hospital emergency parking lot and ran into the emergency room. I was looking all over for someone to help me when I spied Colleen standing in the aisle of the emergency room.

There was no sign of her being hurt, sick, or anything. In fact, she was just standing there all by herself. I ran over to her; she was crying.

"What's wrong?!" I said as I held her in my arms.

She said, "It's the baby, it's Alyssa!"

I looked to my right and there, pale as a ghost, throwing up, and crying, was our little six-month-old Alyssa lying on a gurney. She had a whole team of doctors around her, and blood was everywhere, all over her small arms, and her forehead.

"For heaven's sakes, what is going on?" I asked.

"Alyssa was feeling sickly this morning," Colleen said, "so I took her to see Doctor Bill. Doctor Bill looked her over and sent us home. A few hours later Bill called and told me I had to rush to Mission Hospital with her immediately. He said, 'Don't ask any questions, Colleen, just do as I say.' So I did."

She started to cry. "Honey," she said. "Alyssa is dehydrated, and if they can't get fluids in her she may die!"

"She will be alright!" I said. "We have to trust God, and Doctor

Bill." Then we began to pray as we held each other, watching the doctors and nurses trying to save our baby.

They tried to start an IV on Alyssa, but after too many tries to count, they still could not get one started. Finally, they brought in a surgeon and Colleen and I were asked to step out. I refused and said I wanted to stay and hold her little hand. Doctor Bill got them to let me. They had to cut her little leg open at the ankle and pulled out one of her tiny small veins, but they started that IV and taped her up.

It was a miracle, but we were still not out of the woods. This entire ordeal took about three hours. By now it was getting dark at home, and Tasha and Nick were all alone. Colleen and I left Alyssa asleep in her hospital room, and rushed home, only to find another nightmare in progress. Tasha was trying to take care of Nick, but he was in trouble, too. He was sicker than a dog with diarrhea, as well as throwing up every couple of seconds. Tasha was brave, but when she saw us, she began to sob. I hurriedly picked Nick up and ran to the car with him. We rushed Nick to the hospital emergency room. By now the ER knew us on a first-name basis.

Nick and Alyssa had the same ailment: intestinal gastritis.

They had both lost almost 20% of their body weight and were in terrible danger. Now on top of leukemia, Nick's life was being drained out of him by some stupid intestinal junk. We were getting near the end of our ropes. Colleen called someone from our church to go over to be with Tasha while Colleen and I stayed in the hospital room with Nicky and Alyssa.

Gastritis is very painful, and both babies had diarrhea and were throwing up. Gastritis is also very contagious, thus we had to scrub our hands after each diaper change. Both kids were quarantined together in a glass room, and anyone entering the room had to be gowned, gloved, and masked. Every hour Colleen and I changed about eight diapers apiece. Change the diaper, scrub our hands, change another diaper, wash again, hour after hour. We had to keep the dirty diapers away from their little skin because it was like acid, and it burned their little skin something terrible. Our hands were raw from all the acid and all the scrubbing. The kids screamed and cried and threw up and pooped and screamed some more. It was a living nightmare!

Finally, after we had been fighting this battle for what seemed an eternity, Colleen collapsed on the floor. I yelled for a nurse, and they rushed Colleen to labor and delivery. She was hemorrhaging. The kids kept screaming and dirtying their diapers, and the clock seemed to stand still, and everything seemed to be yelling at me, "NO RELIEF! NO RELIEF!"

I had been awake and running since 3 AM the previous day, and now it was early afternoon on a Saturday. I was scared, beat up, and tired. How were Colleen and the new baby? What was going to happen to Nick and Alyssa? Was Tasha okay? Thought after raging thought, and the hours dragged on, and now it was dark out. I kept changing diapers, the kids kept screaming, and now I could feel myself starting to lose it.

No job! No money! No house! I can't live without Colleen. I don't want to live without Colleen and the kids! "Oh, God, please stop all the screaming!" Diaper after diaper, scrub, scrub. The room was spinning, my hands were raw and burning, Nick was screaming, and Alyssa was crying!

"You are supposed to be the God of our peace!" I yelled. "I don't have any peace here! Where the hell are you???!!!"

I stood there for what seemed like minutes but could have been only seconds. Time was a relative commodity at that point. Suddenly, silence filled the room. It was almost deafening. The kids had fallen asleep and I just stood there. Then the silence was broken, the phone began to ring. I hurriedly grabbed and fumbled with the phone, trying desperately not to wake the kids. It was a nurse from the labor and delivery room.

"We've stopped the bleeding, your wife is stable, and the baby is fine. We're going to keep your wife here for a little while longer to make sure she is stable and then we will be sending her home."

I thanked them for everything; then I hung up the phone. For a second, all was still and quiet. Then the phone rang again. I hadn't taken my hand off the receiver, so I merely lifted my finger off the button, and said, "Hello." It was a lady friend of ours from the church.

"Don't worry, Sam," she said, "everything is under control here at home. I fed Tasha and put her to bed. I am going to stay for as long as you need me to."

I think I thanked her, but I'm not entirely clear what my response was. I do remember hanging up the phone, staring at our two kids sleeping so peacefully in their hospital beds, looking out at the nurse's station, and looking up at the clock in the room thinking to myself, is it 9 AM, or 9 PM? I then sat down for the first time in hours, laid my head back, and fell into a deep sleep.

I must have slept for hours. I was awakened by the tap on the glass windows and the little cooing sounds of Alyssa. Nick was sitting up and saying, "Daddy I'm hungry! Where's Mommy?" I turned at the tapping sound on the window to find 15 of our church friends all laying their hands on the glass smiling and praying, cheering us on. Colleen walked in a few minutes later, looking beautiful as ever. She had big tears in her eyes. She said, "We're going to be okay, Honey! God is with us."

What I learned that night profoundly changed my relationship with God, my wife, and my children. I know it was not a very respectful or wise thing to do, yelling at God as I did, but on the other hand, God became real to me that night, more intimately than ever, there in that hospital room.

God cares for us through all the happenings of our lives! If He knows the number of hairs on our heads, then He indeed is involved in every aspect of our existence. I couldn't fix Nick, I couldn't hold a job, I couldn't avoid eviction, and I couldn't stave off Christmas. I was helpless when Alyssa needed an IV. I couldn't stop the kids from screaming or stop Colleen from hemorrhaging. I was helpless and almost hopeless. It is hard to fathom that God could care so much for me. But He does! Now I don't suggest that you learn this reality by yelling at God, but then again, if that's what it takes for you to realize He is real, shout your loudest. Make it a good one!

We got the kids out of the hospital three days before Christmas.

On Christmas Eve, a family from our church rang our doorbell. When we opened the door we found they had brought us a Christmas tree, a turkey dinner, presents for all the kids, and $50 for Colleen and I, each of us, to buy something for one another. That night we had a feast with their family—what a great Christmas Eve.

Two days after Christmas I found a new job. I started the next Monday.

Less than a week after Christmas we found another house to rent, and the new landlord gave us a break. He let us move in on New

Year's Day, and we didn't have to pay him until the 15th of the month; which happened to coincide with the coming of my first paycheck. Fifteen guys from our church came to move us, and within two hours we were out of the old house and into the new. Late in January, only a month after our overwhelming hopeless ordeal, Colleen gave birth to our baby son Travis.

And the best Christmas present of all: on Christmas Eve we received a phone call from the head of Nick's medical team, from CHOC Hospital.

"I've got some good news," he said. "I know its late, but I thought you'd want to know, it's not leukemia. We discovered Nick has a rare blood disorder called cyclic neutropenia. You will have to monitor him a bit through the natural kid sickness times. Pump him with vitamins, feed him Mom's good home cooking, make sure he gets lots of rest and proper exercise. He should grow out of this condition and be just fine."

We were going to be alright.

CHAPTER 7

Let's talk about work. Though I haven't said it outright yet, you may have noticed that the singing in a nightclub thing stopped working out for me and I had to get a reasonable job so I could provide for my family. It was okay to chase that career when it was just me, but now that I had other people to take care of, I had to wise up, put the singing dream on the back burner, and find something that would do more than make ends meet.

But that's easier said than done. I had a tough time maintaining a job. I didn't do anything wrong; it's just that I couldn't find my niche. I was searching and searching and Colleen never discouraged me but always encouraged me. She'd help me look for jobs, and if I got fired, she'd say, "That's okay, they don't understand what they've got. It's their loss, don't worry about it. You'll find another job."

And I did. I kept finding jobs, but it seemed like I couldn't hold a position, and so I was trying to find my calling. Finally I got a job as a salesperson, and I worked my way up to being a sales manager. Sales were good, and I ended up working up the ladder to being a sales director and finally started making some excellent money.

I eventually landed a job with a national behavioral health medical corporation, working in a community relations and marketing position. Behavioral health is a field that works with people fighting addictions and depression, and I marketed services to hospitals like psychiatrists and psychologists where disturbed people could hopefully get some hope and help.

The hospitals and clinics I worked for were filled with psychiatric sociologists, psychologists, sociologists, counselors, and, obviously, patients. My responsibility was to find the people who needed help. It was a Christian program that would market to churches, mental health professionals, schools, and people who were having problems. The program was hospital-based for inpatient care.

I mainly worked with youth; it was a youth unit with thirty-six beds, and my responsibility was to keep the beds occupied, which I did. The place was full and a lot of neat things were going on—people were getting the help they needed—and it was great, and I loved the program.

But I kept having a run-in with one of the administrators of the units, and she had an issue with me. Anyway, one thing led to another where she wanted me to be more accountable than I'd ever been to anybody and write down what I did every minute of the day.

She'd call me on the carpet for all kinds of stuff. I don't think she liked me very much, and even though the unit was full, she always gave me a hard time.

Finally, another company came to me and asked if I'd come work for them, promising me a big budget, an office, and all the lovely trimmings. Best of all, they made me a reasonable offer for my compensation to where I'd be making about twice what I was making already, and without all the hassle.

I took the job.

It was a secular company, but they were opening a Christian unit. I was going to be the Operations Director and Marketing Director for that unit, and at first, it was wonderful. But I realized pretty quickly that the administrator of the secular program was actually over everything, including our Christian-focused unit. He didn't like Christians and, I think, didn't like that the company was trying to get into that market by marketing to Christians.

And so, the big budget I originally had was cut in half. Then, just as I would get the marketing plan set up for radio advertising, TV advertising, pamphlets, flyers, whatever, he'd come back and cut it in half again. Cut, trim, cut. He kept cutting my budget until finally we only had about five patients in a forty-bed unit.

Despite all these setbacks, I was still kind of the golden boy of the corporation. They had high hopes for the Christian market, and I worked eighty-hour weeks at ten or fifteen hours a day to try to make those hopes come true. One day I came home, and Travis, our youngest boy—he was about five at the time—met me at the door as I opened it up.

He looked up at me and said, "Who are you?"

"I'm your daddy."

"Oh, I didn't recognize you."

Then he turned around and walked into the kitchen. I followed him in and saw all the kids were sitting around the table while Colleen was standing at the stove making dinner. I walked over to give her a little kiss on the cheek, but she was kind of cold to me, and I didn't know why. I hadn't done anything wrong, I thought. And the kids were kind of cool to me, too.

Finally, I said, "Honey, what's wrong? What's going on with everybody? How come everybody's so cold to me?" But she didn't say anything; she just kept cooking.

"Honey! Honey, what's wrong?"

Colleen laid down what she was doing for a second and turned to me and said, "Sam Parsons, you're going to die a rich, lonely old man without a wife or kids. But you can keep going if you want to."

Then she turned around and got back to cooking.

"What are you talking about?" I said. I was so clueless!

She finally laid down her spoon again, turned to me, and said, "You're gone in the morning before anyone gets up. You don't get home till after dark, till everybody's in bed. On the weekends you're nothing but a zombie. But you keep going. And you're making lots of money, and you're really important, but you're going to lose your wife and kids over this thing. We don't care about the money—we care about you."

Then she went back to the stove. The rest of the evening was cold; the kids didn't mistreat me or anything—they weren't mean, they were just cool like I was a stranger to them and not their dad.

I went to bed that night and it was like sleeping with an ice cube. Colleen didn't want anything to do with me.

I didn't sleep very well that night. I went downstairs and read my Bible the next morning like I usually did. But I just started crying before the Lord, I was on my knees and crying, saying, "Lord, I'm about to lose my family. I don't know what to do. I realize I'm stuck in a squirrel cage."

I thought I was working for my family, but the truth is that I was working for my ego. I was important, and I had people answering to me, I was a boss and all that other junk; I was just beside myself, I was stuck. We had bills to pay, and I was stuck.

So I sat there crying for a long time, and finally Colleen and the kids came downstairs. They found me a mess. I hadn't left for work yet, which was different. I was sitting in the chair, still in my pajamas.

"Daddy, what are you doing here?" they asked.

"I'm not going to work today."

"Are you sick?"

"No." I called them all over and opened up. "Daddy's stuck in a squirrel cage, and I can't get out. I don't know what to do. I don't know how *not* to work. And I'm lost, I don't know what to do, I'm just...lost."

I was just sitting there crying, and they were concerned, they started hugging me and stuff, and so I said, "I need you guys to pray for me. That Daddy would get out of the squirrel cage."

I don't think the kids knew what was going on, but Colleen of course knew.

"I need prayer really bad," I said. So they all prayed over me, and especially my beautiful wife, she prayed over me. We cried, but I didn't know what to do. Fortunately, the answer to all our prayers came a couple of weeks later.

My boss knew I played music because I'd take my guitar and play sometimes at lunch and stuff for the Christian patients, so he said, "I need you to fill in for something, for the morning slot before the therapists get here. You don't have any patients to speak of, so I need you to go to the secular unit, and I need you to sing to the patients. Just keep them busy until the therapists come here; I don't care what you sing, just keep them busy."

He was my boss, and I didn't have a lot of patients, and I didn't want to lose my job or any more of my budgets, so I did what he asked. I went upstairs to the unit where the patients were. These patients were having problems, they would smoke two packs of cigarettes before 8:00 in the morning and drink two pots of coffee each.

There were about twenty or thirty people up there, and so I sang and played old rock and roll songs—the ones I used to do in the nightclubs. I'm a pretty good guitar player, so I impressed them with my guitar-playing. They'd sit and listen, and after the first day I thought, *You know what? I'm just playing. I'm not doing any good; I'm not ministering to these people.*

So the next day I decided to sing some rock and roll but add in the first step of the twelve-step program. I was just going to reword it a little bit. So I went in and said, "I've come to realize that my life is unmanageable, due to sin. Not alcohol, not drugs, but sin." I explained to them what sin was, "You're missing the mark. You aren't living up to God's perfect plan for you."

I taught them about the theological question of missing the mark.

Then the next day I went out, and I decided I'd do it again, and it felt pretty good, playing and singing again.

I started asking them questions, and they began sharing their questions with me. I knew my Bible pretty well at that time—I read it all the time, and I'd been studying for ministry—and so I'd answer questions. And we talked about stuff, and it was actually a pretty good deal, and so I thought it was fine.

One day after I wrapped up sharing with them, I went down to my office and hadn't been in there very long before heard a knock on the door. There, standing in my doorway, was a young man named Mike.

"I want to know more about Jesus," he said.

I invited him in, and we talked for a few minutes, and the next thing I knew we were on the floor, on our knees, and he was praying to accept Christ. I was like, *Wow, that's...wow, that's good.*

The next day I went back upstairs to talk and share again. Afterward, I went back down to my office. Once again, I heard a knock on the door. This time, it was five people who came down all at the same time to accept Christ. On bended knees, they gave their hearts to Christ.

And again I thought, *Wow.*

So I go back up the next day, and before I even got finished doing my group, the administrator called me into his office.

"I don't want you doing any of that salvation stuff with the patients," he said. "You have to stop it."

"I don't know if I *can* stop it," I said. "You wanted me to do the best I could do, and that's the best I can do."

So he and I had a little confrontation about that.

The next day I showed up to work and found out that I had been locked out of my office. They called me in and told me they were closing the Christian unit and they fired all the Christians—27 of us in all.

That was on the 30th of December, which means it was right after Christmas when I got laid off. So it was a hard time. They called it "reduction of force," and we were all out on our ears.

I didn't know what to do. I mean, here I'd gone in early almost every day, at 5:00 or 5:30 every morning, and I'd walk the unit, anointing every room in the Christian unit with oil and praying over it. I poured my heart and soul into the job, but though it didn't know it at the time, the "reduction of force" was an answer to my squirrel cage prayer.

I remembered a phone call I had had with my old music business friend, Jesse, about six months earlier. Jesse and I were catching up over the phone, and she said to me, "Sam, I've been thinking. If you had all the time and the money in the world, what would you do with yourself?"

"Well, that's a stupid question, Jesse," I said. "I'll never have that kind of time or money."

"Let's just say you won the $50 million lotto, and after you've taken all your vacations and bought your boats and junk and homes and stuff, what would you want to do with your life? What would get you out of bed in the morning? What would you do? What would propel you through your day?"

"I don't know," I said. "I never thought of it"

It was a simple question but I'd never considered it.

"I guess I could think about it," I said, "but right now I'm too busy."

Jesse pressed me to promise to pray about it and take a look at it, and I humored her, but that was about it. The next morning, I woke up to do my regular Bible time, and I prayed about it and prayed about it. And I did that the next day and the next until finally, I realized what I would do. And I settled it.

Here it was, six months later. I was newly laid off and I had to go home and tell Colleen that I was laid off again. I didn't know what it was going to take to get another job. It was pretty frustrating. I'd been leading worship in a little inner city church every week, and I respected the pastor—Pastor Rich—so instead of going home first, I went over to see Pastor Rich because I didn't know what I was going to do with myself.

I told Pastor Rich, "I'm sick of this corporate America stuff. They sell the company, or something else happens, or politics, and it's just driving me crazy."

Pastor Rich looked at me and sincerely asked this question: "Sam, if you had all the time and the money in the world what would you do with yourself?"

Almost word for word what Jesse had asked six months earlier!

At first, I just looked at him stunned that he said the same words. Then I said, "Well, I figured it out. I know what I would do."

"What did you come up with?"

"I'd sing for people and share my love of the Lord with them."

"So, what's stopping you?" he said.

"What do you mean, what's stopping me?" I said.

"Well, you don't have a job now, so what do you have to lose? Why don't you do that?"

"Who would I sing for? Everybody's at work."

He thought for a moment. "Let's back up a second," he said. "Would you sing day or night?"

"What do you mean?"

"Pick one. Would you like to go out and sing in the night or would you rather sing during the day?"

"I guess if I could pick, then I'd sing during the day because then I'd get to be home with my wife and kids at night."

"Okay," he said, "let's go down that road for a minute. Who's home in the daytime you could sing for?"

"I don't know; everybody's working."

"Wait a second," he said. "What about the kids in schools? Why couldn't you go out and do a program for schools, and do a program for kids?"

"Gosh, I'm not really a kid person," I said. "I mean, I love my kids, but I don't think I'm a kid entertainer. I don't think I know how to do that."

"Okay, what about old people?"

"What do you mean by old people?"

"Retired people."

"Well, they're all in Winnebagos, they're all playing golf and fishing and traveling and stuff."

"No, not all of them. Some of them live in homes."

"We all live in homes."

"No, I'm talking about nursing homes. Retirement homes, hospitals, places like that."

I paused for a moment. "I never thought of that."

"There's a nursing home right down the corner here," he said. "Why don't you go down there and sing for them?"

"Right now?"

"Yeah, right now!"

I always take my guitar with me almost everywhere I go. I keep it in the trunk of my car, just in case I need it. So I said, "Okay, but I don't know what I'll sing."

"Don't drive down there," Pastor Rich said. "You walk and pray about it on the way. I think God will tell you what to sing."

So I grabbed my guitar and started walking down the street, praying the whole way. I got to the nursing home and opened up the door, and it had the longest hallway in the world, it felt like it was five miles long.

I walked in and looked down this long hallway. I went to the nurse's station, where one of the nurses looked at me and said, "Can I help you?"

I knew it would sound silly, but I said, "I came to sing for your people."

She started laughing! "Okay, my people are all the way at the end of the hall, the last door on your right."

I took my guitar case and walked down that long hallway to the last room on the right. As I walked into the room, there was a young lady with her back to the door and a lot of older ladies sitting around, and she was doing their nails. Cleaning their nails and polishing their nails and stuff like that, and they started pointing to me and saying things to her.

She turned around and she saw me and she said, "Can I help you?"

"I'm here to sing for your people."

"Okay, go ahead," and she turned around and started back on

their nails.

I'm standing there dumbfounded, so I took my guitar out of my case, and I was still trying to think of what to sing. I remember seeing the movie *The Jazz Singer* with Neil Diamond, and in the middle of the film he was running away, trying to find himself and grow a beard, all that stuff.

In the movie, he walks into this bar carrying his guitar, and the bartender says, "Can you play that?"

And he says, "Yeah."

"Can you play 'You Are My Sunshine?'"

And so Neil Diamond plays "You Are My Sunshine."

So I thought that was a good start. If it was good enough for Neil Diamond, it was good enough for me, and I played "You Are My Sunshine." And before I was finished with that song, I thought of another song my grandfather used to sing, so I played "Let Me Call You Sweetheart" next. And after that I sang "Home On The Range," and then I don't know, I just started singing old songs that I grew up listening to and singing. Songs that my grandmother and grandfather used to sing with all their friends, back when we'd all sit around and play guitar on the porch on Friday nights.

I sang for about 45 minutes, and when I had finished, the lady doing nails said, "You're pretty good. Would you like to come back?"

"Yeah, I guess so."

"How much do you charge?"

I never thought about charging, so I said, "I don't know. Whatever you give me."

"I'll give you $25 each time you come. Call me tomorrow, and I'll give you a regular monthly schedule."

I walked back to the church, but instead of going inside, I just stood there, confused by the whole thing. It happened so fast. I packed up my guitar, drove home, and told Colleen the news about being laid off.

"Don't worry, Honey," she said, "They don't know what they lost. You'll find another job. God will give us another job, don't worry."

Then I told her what happened with Pastor Rich. I told her what he said, and what I did, and all about the singing.

"Do you think God is in it?" she asked.

"I don't know, but I haven't got a job right now, I haven't got anything to lose."

"What are you going to do?"

"I think I'll print up a bunch of résumés and send them out to the contacts I have and try to get a marketing job, and in the meantime, while I'm waiting, I think I'll just go out and find places to sing."

"Okay," she said. "I guess we'll see if God's in it."

I woke up the next morning, and this idea hit me to open the phonebook and look up *old folks homes*. But they're not listed under that! It was under *convalescent homes/skilled nursing homes*. At any rate, I wrote down about a dozen places. I decided I was going to map out a route, and I was going to go to about five homes a day. So that became my daily routine. I'd walk into a place, take out my guitar, and sing. I don't know if you've ever been in sales, but I had a 100% close ratio. I went to 80 nursing homes, and all 80 asked me to come back. I mean not one of them said no!

I was like, "Wow!" And a couple of the places gave me an honorarium for even coming in to audition. They all paid, and a few of them also gave me about $40.

I lined up about 80 places to play and that sounded great. I had a whole plan to schedule out the entire day playing music. The problem is that you can't work it out that way; the residents wake up late, they go to bed early, they've got lunchtime in the middle. In terms of time you can play music for them, they have about three hours in the morning and two or three in the afternoon, so I could only play about four or five places a day.

The first month I made $400. I don't know how we survived on $400, but we did. In Matthew 6:33 it says, "Seek first his kingdom of righteousness and all these things will be added to you."

It says in Psalms 37:40 "Delight in the Lord and he'll give you the desires of your heart."

I've been playing music for years; I've been singing all my life. But this was different. I didn't get a lot of applause, because a lot of them were physically incapable of it! But I kept singing; I'd go from one song to the next. I sang old hymns and country and rock and folk.

I was delighting in God, that He was making a way for me to sing. And that whole time I kept waiting on calls for my "normal" marketing career, sending out résumés and trying to get a job, but I never heard back.

So I just kept singing.

We were struggling. Boy, were we struggling. Colleen and I did without food two, maybe three days a week. We'd feed the kids, but we'd go without food. But we just kept going.

I look back on it now, and my wife never complained. Never. She just kept encouraging me, "Go out and bless someone." People would give their life to Christ, and I'd come home, and we would rejoice. It was amazing. It was very humbling but very amazing.

Colleen just kept saying, "God's our provider. Let's just stay the course." That's what she'd say to me. "Let's just seek ye first His kingdom."

After struggling for a few months, it was pretty hard. Somebody told me I should start writing a newsletter to get donations. I started a newsletter and Colleen would edit it. I think there'd be more red ink than black ink on it because she'd edit it very enthusiastically. "You have to change it," she would say, "you can't keep it that way." We'd argue about it, but she was always right, and it would be about ten times better after she touched it. Everything she touched was beautiful. Beautiful.

I got tired of not making enough money and of not having health insurance. And I was getting frustrated. One day I showed up at a hospital where I sang regularly. The floors on the unit I normally would sing on were being cleaned. So, the activity director, Cliff, said, "Sam do you mind going down to Station D?"

That was the AIDS and cancer ward. "Okay," I said. "I've never been down to Station D."

"Everybody in there is terminal, and nobody wants to go in there," he said, "but would you mind doing it?"

I didn't mind at all. I went down to Station D and started singing.

I went into one of the first rooms, and there was a man whose face had been eaten away by cancer. I was trying to share the Lord with him and sing for him, but he just scoffed at me. As I started to leave the room, his roommate, a guy lying in a bed reading paper, laid the paper down and said: "I've never heard anything like that before." And you know, in America, you think that people have at least heard a sermon, but this guy had never heard anything.

I said, "Okay, let me share it with you." I explained how man had fallen and that there was sin, and that there was no way to be close to the pure God when we are covered in sin but that God chose a way to save man from his sin, and that He sent His Son to die on the cross.

"But," I said, "it takes faith. It's impossible to please God without faith." And so I walked him through it. And lo and behold, he gave his life to Christ! I was so excited. I keep Bibles in my car, so I ran down to the parking lot, grabbed a Bible and took it back to him. I highlighted a few verses and prayed over him and gave him the Bible. I told Cliff, the Activity Director, what had happened and about the man getting salvation, then I left.

As I left I thought to myself, *We're so poor and broke; I just have to find a new job. I can't do this anymore. I'm gonna find a real job.*

I picked up the newspaper that Sunday morning to see if I could find a real job. I was scheduled to go back on Monday to the same hospital I had visited on Friday. As I arrived, I ran into Cliff.

He said, "Sam, you won't believe what happened. That guy that you led to Christ on Friday had an orderly put him in a wheelchair and wheel him up and down to every room of Station D, and he preached the gospel and said 'I'm going to heaven. I'm not dying without hope. I gave my heart to Jesus.'"

He preached up and down the hallway for an hour.

"Sam, he died that very night."

And right then, the Lord spoke to my heart, and said:

"I've got you right where I want you. This is your work. I will provide."

It turned my life around.

I went home and told Colleen what had happened, and we both just wept.

"Honey we've got to stay the course," she said.

And of course, that's when I finally got a job offer.

A company called me, a behavioral health company that had been my competitor before. I still thought I needed a real job, so I went in for an interview, and I guess they liked me because they offered me an office, a company car, an excellent salary, and all the things that I thought I needed. I had on my three-piece suit, ready to go to work; I could start on Monday. I didn't see that I was about to sign up for the squirrel cage again.

I was listening to him talk about all the benefits, a 401(k) and health insurance, everything we needed and I wanted, and I heard the Lord say to me:

"I already gave you a job."

I sat there for a minute and thought about it. So I looked at the guy—he was a Christian guy, it was a Christian company—and I said "I don't mean to waste your time. I know you're going to find the right guy, but I am not the right guy. As you were talking, the Lord spoke to my heart and told me that He's already given me a job."

I told him what my job was, about the man who had died, and he said, "Well, praise the Lord."

"Yeah," I said.

"Let's pray," he said, and he put his arm on my shoulder and prayed for me. It was amazing. But when I left, I was a little nervous. I was going to have to go back home and tell Colleen, you know, about how I'd turned down the salary and all those benefits.

So I went home, and I said, "Honey I need to talk to you."

We sat down, and I held her hands, and she said, "Just please tell me you didn't take the job."

"I thought you wanted me to take the job!"

"I do. I hate this. I'm scared all the time," she said. "But you can get another job; you can't get another God. You have do what God's called you to do."

And so, we lived our lives like that. God would tell her the same thing He told me. You know we had to do it that way.

Not long after that, I got a call from my friend Don. He and his wife Grace had supported me as a worship leader for that small inner city church I had led worship for. He had donated the $300 salary I earned leading worship there, which helped out a great deal.

Colleen and I were still working through the trenches, but we had a ministry God had called us to. I had left that small church to pursue the nursing home ministry full-time.

Don called me up and asked me out to lunch. At that lunch, Don told me straight out that he was going to give us $2,000 a month. $2,000 was like a million dollars to us. We weren't making anything close to that.

Then, to make sure I understood, he handed me a check for $2,000.

"We are going to support you," he said. "I believe in what you're doing. How you're trying to lead people to Christ and how you love people. I believe in you."

I went home and told Colleen what had happened. And the kids were sitting there at the table, and they started jumping up and down and saying, "We can climb trees! We can climb trees!"

Colleen started crying.

"What's that about?" I asked.

"I wouldn't let the kids ride skateboards or climb trees because we didn't have health insurance for them," she said. "All the other kids would climb trees but they couldn't. I told them they couldn't ride skateboards until we got insurance and maybe if Daddy comes home with enough money we could get insurance."

They were thrilled.

Gosh, the sacrifices she made for me. I used to call her up on the phone, and I'd thank her, for sacrificing for me. Cause I love what I get to do. And it was amazing. She was amazing.

CHAPTER 8

Colleen and I were perfect for each other because we both would do anything for ministry. We didn't get to take many vacations, but one time we decided we could go down to Temecula, which was an hour and a half south, and rent a little hotel and go wine-tasting. We'd never done that, but we thought it'd be fun, and we'd heard that Temecula was close.

We had it all planned out and the time had finally arrived for our little getaway. We were getting ready that night to leave the next morning. I was downstairs reading my Bible, while the kids were asleep and Colleen was upstairs finishing her packing. All of a sudden the phone rang: it was Colleen's sister, Connie, calling from her home in Las Vegas.

Her husband, John, had gone off the deep end. He had a gun and was threatening to kill himself. So Connie called, just petrified. She and her two little boys were locked in the bedroom while her husband was downstairs with a pistol screaming that he's going to kill himself and that he's going to kill them.

I mean, it was just scary. So I go up to talk to Colleen to tell her what's going on, and she said, "What are we going to do?" We didn't have an answer.

At that time John was just crazy, and I thought, Well, let him shoot himself. Let him go ahead. Let him kill himself. I mean, good riddance. I know that's terrible, but he wasn't a real good husband to Connie, and he'd treated Colleen's mom and her stepdad awful as well. I didn't think much of the guy.

So I went downstairs and reopened my Bible, and I'm reading in Proverbs 24, where it says to "Stand in the way of those that are being led to slaughter."

We're to deliver those people.

We couldn't say to God, "I was unmindful of this," because God knows our heart.

I read that and I felt so convicted because I didn't have compassion for John. Or Connie either, I guess.

I took my Bible upstairs and read that passage to Colleen.

"We're going to Vegas, aren't we?" she said.

"I think we have to."

"Yeah, we have to," she said. "We have to."

So we got someone to stay with the kids, then got in the car immediately and drove to Vegas, and we made it in record time. I think we made it in four hours.

We got there in the middle of the night and John was still sitting down there, drunk, with this gun.

He let us in the house, and while Colleen ran upstairs to be with Connie and the boys, I sat down and started talking to John.

"You know I could kill you in a second," he said.

"Yeah, but the difference between you and me, John, is that, if you kill me, I win. I go to heaven. But if anything happens to you, you don't."

I shared the love of Christ with him, as much as I could.

I don't remember how it happened, but over the course of an hour of talking, John ended up on his knees, in my arms, in tears. He handed me the gun, sobbing and giving his heart to Jesus. Connie and Colleen came downstairs; the boys were asleep, John cried and apologized to Connie. We stayed and talked through some things and by the time we were finished it was about midday the following day. They were hugging as we left. We felt like it was pretty safe, so we decided to head down to Temecula anyway.

We took off from Vegas and drove, and we were so tired because we had been up so long. We got to our destination, and it was getting kind of dark, so we pulled over at Del Taco to take a break. We just laid our heads back and slept for three or four hours.

Colleen woke up, and she says in that perfect Colleen timing,

"Y'know, you take me to the nicest places, sleeping in Del Taco parking lots."

Oh, but I'm not sorry we went. It was the right thing to do, and it was good ministry.

We put up with a lot of interruptions. Now, this is probably a tacky story to tell, but it's funny. Colleen and I had been way too busy for a couple of weeks. I had been ministering, had presided over a couple of funerals and a wedding, led worship for a church that week and had been to all twenty of my nursing homes.

It was early Saturday morning, and Colleen came to me and said, "Honey, you know we haven't been together 'romantically' for a while. I think if you get the yard work done early enough maybe we can watch a movie with the kids and can get them down early."

Those of you who are married know what it means to "get the kids down early." And, man, that was all I needed to hear! I mowed the lawn in, like, fifteen minutes. I wanted the kids to go to bed at 2:30 in the afternoon! So I go up, and I shower, I get cleaned up, and she puts on a movie for the kids. I put on her favorite shirt of mine, and her favorite cologne and I go downstairs, and I'm looking at her, and she's looking at me, and I'm like, "Hey baby," and we're making little goo-goo eyes, and the kids are watching the movie.

Finally, it comes time to put the kids down to bed, and we put them down to bed, and they did not want to go to sleep, but they finally drifted off.

And then the phone rings.

It was my friend Dan. "My brother Ray is dying," he said. "He doesn't know the Lord, and he's at Kaiser hospital. I need you right now."

Well, man, the last thing I wanted to do was go to a hospital! I was looking forward to being with my girl!

But Colleen said, "Honey when God calls you, you've got to go."

"Yeah I know, I know. But. Gosh."

"Honey, you have to go, there's no questioning. You have to go."

"Okay," I said. "I'll hurry back."

So I hurried on the toll road, driving about 90 miles an hour, and I got to Kaiser Hospital. Normally when I visit a person in the hospital, I walk in, take out my guitar, and sing them two or three songs. I try to get a real good atmosphere happening. And then I'd softly say, "How's your faith holding up? What's going on?" That's what I'd normally do.

But this time I was in a hurry, so I got in, and I didn't even take my guitar out of my case; I just watched the nurses work on Ray, pumping some antibiotics into him. He was laying on the bed, and realized I had never met Ray. On one side was Dan and on the other side of the bed was Ray and Dan's mother, Donna.

"This is Sam," Dan said as the nurses finished their work.

I looked at Ray, and said, "Ray, it's looking pretty bad for you right now."

Dan looked at me, and then Donna looked at me.

"Looks like they're counting you out, buddy."

Ray just kind of shook his head, and Dan and Donna were looking like, *What are you doing?*

"But you're okay, man, you're going to be good. You've given your heart to Jesus; you're going to go to heaven. So I think everything's right with the world."

Ray just looked at me like a deer in the headlights.

"You *have* surrendered your heart to Christ, right?" I said.

"No."

"Oh, okay. Well, Ray, right now you are on a train headed straight to hell, and you're not gonna like it. There's gnashing of teeth and wailing; there's sadness. It's un-stinkin'-believable. You're not going to want to go there. Now you can go there if you want to, but if it were me, I'd switch trains."

I paused for a minute.

"What do you think, Ray?"

Well, Dan looked at me like, *Sam what are you doing?*

Donna was looking at him like, *Why did you bring this crazy man in here?*

But Ray looked at me and said, "I want to switch trains."

And I said, "Well, let me tell you how it works, Ray." So I shared the gospel.

"I want to give my heart to Jesus," Ray said.

"I can't guarantee it will heal you, though," I said. "He might. I can't guarantee it, Ray. But I can guarantee if you surrender your heart to Christ you'll go to heaven. You will not go to hell."

"I want to go to heaven so bad," Ray said.

"Okay. Let's pray."

I got so excited that we prayed. We started laughing, and I pulled out my guitar. And we sang for forty-five minutes, and we had a good time. Finally, I packed up the guitar, and I went to my car just weeping all the way thinking, *Oh Lord, I almost missed it. I was so in my agenda, not yours.*

I called up Colleen on the phone and told her what had happened, and she rejoiced. She just laughed and cried on the phone.

"Oh honey, that is such good news," she said.

"I know. I feel so embarrassed because I almost missed it."

"But you're just like the guy in the story Jesus told, you were the obedient son, even though you didn't want to do, you did it. We have to be obedient."

And then she said the best thing: "I'm still awake, and I'm waiting for you."

I think I drove a hundred and twenty miles an hour on the way home.

CHAPTER 9

Colleen Parsons was the absolute one and only true love of my life, forever and ever. I adored her. She was perfect for me in absolutely every way. Proverbs 18:22 says, "He who finds a wife finds a good thing," and I found a *great* thing. I had the best wife that ever walked on the face of this Earth. I am devastated without her, and the tug of heaven is always pulling me towards her.

Every time she turned around, she looked for the Lord. She tried to find the Lord in everything. There was one Christmas when she and I were doing the dishes. I had bought a roll-out basketball hoop for the kids, and they were all out in the front playing basketball. We had just finished Christmas dinner, so the table was a mess, and there was wrapping paper everywhere.

I looked over at her and said, "Boy, Christmas went quick."

"I think Christmas went too quickly," she said. "I wonder if it's worth it. I mean we did all these gifts, and now the paper is everywhere. It just seems like Christmas is over too soon. You almost fell off the roof hanging the house lights, and now it's over."

"I know, I feel the same way. What can we do?"

"I don't know."

A month later, we finally decided to have a family meeting about Christmas and talk to the kids. So we gathered everyone and said, "You know, Christmas just came and went way too quickly this year. Does anyone else think the same?

"Yeah."

"What can we do to make it last longer?"

The kids thought for a minute.

"We can turn on *White Christmas* sooner." That was Travis's favorite movie.

"We could turn the air conditioning down."

"We could put frost on the windows."

"We could put up the tree in October."

Then finally Nick said, "Daddy, we could go to a nursing home on Christmas and give out presents and stuff. You know, like you do every day. We could do that."

Everybody stopped and took it in. Someone suggested we could take our dog Jack; someone else suggested we could give gifts and candy canes; someone else suggested we could sing, and Nick could play the guitar and Travis could play his bongos.

I put it to a vote, and it was unanimous.

So that's what we planned for the next Christmas and every Christmas afterward. It became a new family tradition. Throughout the year, Colleen would buy lovely little gifts at the dollar store or Big Lots, or at some big sale she'd see. We would have a big wrapping party to wrap the gifts, and when Christmas came, we hit the road running. We did our family stuff in the morning and then headed out to the homes around noon. We walked the halls and sang while the kids gave out gifts. And it was the best thing about Christmas for us. It was wonderful.

Christmas night at the dinner table we would always talk about everything we saw that day. Colleen would stay up on Christmas Eve night making Christmas dinner and getting all the presents ready, and we'd put them in the car and then we'd go to bed. The next morning the kids would all open up their gifts, and then we'd head out and come home where Colleen would warm up Christmas dinner.

Logistically we had to figure out a new way to do Christmas, but the kids liked it, and we had a great time. Every year it was terrific. We did it every year, and we still do it every year.

It's going to be a little different this year with Colleen gone. But it will still be good. She loved it so much!

I remember one Christmas; it looked like we had a million gifts so almost every day that December I'd grab a few gifts to take out with me to the homes or hospitals I visited. All the gifts were in a large furniture box, hundreds of them. I thought. But what I didn't know was the number of presents in that box was deceptive—the bottom of the box was filled not with little gifts but about ten full-size blankets.

Christmas morning when we got ready to leave, the kids and I counted the gifts, and there were only about seventy-five, and we were going to a hundred-bed unit. That's when I discovered the blankets. We needed twenty-five more gifts! So, while Colleen was getting ready, I panicked. I had the kids looking for things to wrap up for gifts; I'm taking stuff off shelves, the kids are finding stuff, and we are using all the wrapping paper from the floor to wrap everything we can get our hands on. By that point, we probably had about eighty-five gifts maybe, and I'm thinking, *Oh gosh.*

Colleen came down, and we packed up the gifts in the car, and Alyssa, our baby girl, said, "Dad, what are we going to do?"

I replied with my great, manly, God voice. "Oh, the Lord will provide." But I had no clue what we were going to do and was just hoping that maybe some people weren't there, and maybe there would only be eighty-five people.

We got to the nursing home we'd chosen and started walking the halls and singing, having a good time and ministering to people. The kids were singing and playing, going up and down the halls. And of course we were giving out gifts; Colleen kept reaching in the bag and pulling out gift after gift. It was enjoyable, just like always.

We were almost done when a nurse was coming on duty to start her shift, and I asked Colleen if we had any more gifts. She reached in, pulled out the last gift, and said, "We have one more!" We gave it to that nurse and started walking out to the parking lot.

"Honey, which beds didn't get gifts?" I asked Colleen.

"What are you talking about?" she said. She wasn't putting me on—she really didn't know what I meant.

"Some of the people who weren't there didn't get a gift because we didn't have enough. Which beds were they?"

"Honey, everybody got a gift. I even gave one to the kitchen staff and a couple of doctors."

"You couldn't have."

"Honey, I did."

I told her how we counted and knew we weren't starting with enough gifts for all the people we'd meet.

"Honey, every time I reached in, there was a gift."

We counted it up and figured we had given away probably 115 gifts. And I knew we only had eighty-five, I counted.

It was, quite literally, a Christmas miracle.

My girl was so committed to the Lord. She made me ten times a better man because of that. She raised the bar and, boy, sometimes it was hard to keep up with her. She had it pretty high. One of my favorite stories about that was the time Jerry, our future son-in-law, came to us to ask for Tasha's hand in marriage.

They'd been dating a while, and it was apparent they were head over heels in love with each other. So we knew this day was coming, but we were a little troubled because Jerry didn't know Christ. When the appointed time came for him to make his request, we sat in the family room, with Jerry on the couch and Colleen and I together in my easy chair.

"I've come to ask for Tasha's hand in marriage," he said, "and I'd like your blessing."

So it was one of those times, those magical times when you say things right. You know, a lot of times you go to say things and when it's over you think *Oh, I wish I'd have said something else; I should have mentioned that instead.* But this was one of those times where God gave us exactly the right words.

The inner strength of my wife, I could just feel her praying. So I know that's why it worked, she was praying the whole time I'd say the right thing. You see, she was such a strong girl. She was such a subservient, wonderful wife, and when I say *subservient,* I mean she held the bar high; she made me jump for it. She was tougher than nails, but she always showed me a standard and believed in me. Always.

"Do you know what you're asking?" I said.

"I'm asking for her hand in marriage," Jerry said.

"But you said you want our blessing."

"Yeah."

"Well, let me tell you what a blessing looks like from a Christian father and mother. Here's what I believe." I shared my faith, and then I said, "Jerry, you've never surrendered your heart to Christ. So what you're really asking is if I'm willing to let you break my wife's heart and my heart."

He just looked like a deer in the headlights, and he said, "I wouldn't...I'm not asking for that."

"Well, you don't mean to. You wouldn't do that; you're a good boy. I think she's made a good choice in you, but, son, you wouldn't mean to do it but you would. You'll break my heart, and you'll break my wife's heart. And I protect my wife's heart with all I've got.

"This is how it works, Jerry: if you become our son-in-law, we don't look at it as a son-in-law, we look at it as a son. We take you into our family, and everything from the time you're married, from that day forward, every decision we make, we'll have you in mind. And we're going to pray for you every day, and the more and more we get to know you, we're going to fall deeper and deeper in love with you.

"And then one day, because we're older, we will both die. And as I'm laying on my deathbed and you come to say goodbye, I will be saying goodbye to you for the last time because you're not headed for heaven. At that moment, my heart will break because I'll never see you again. Am I willing to let you break my wife's heart like that? Or my heart like that?

"So, this is a big decision, it's not a light decision, and I know you love Tasha and I know she loves you. But this is a big decision that mother and I have to pray about."

"Okay," he said, and then he started to get up to leave.

"No, Jerry, you don't have to leave," I said. Then Colleen and I got on our knees and faced each other. We wrapped our arms around each other—oh, I miss that—and we looked in each other's eyes and prayed.

She gave me that look.

Oh, I miss that look.

And I said, "Okay, we're willing."

I know Jerry was taken aback, and we didn't mean to shock him so much, but it was serious. He's my son, and I do love him.

About six weeks later, I was leading worship at church, and my kids were there, and Jerry was there, too, and so we get to the end of the service, and the pastor did an altar call, asking anyone who wanted to come up and accept Christ. I was on stage, playing my guitar softly behind him. I had my eyes closed, just praying—I was probably praying for Jerry, actually—pleading, "Somebody, Lord, open up a heart and come into a heart, take residence in a heart. Salvation is such a wonderful thing, and everybody needs it."

At the end of the altar call, we finished the song, and my bass player leaned over and said, "Sam, you know your daughter's boyfriend stood up when the pastor asked who wanted to give their heart to Christ?"

"Really?" I was thrilled! I put my guitar on the guitar stand and left the stage and walked over to Jerry and I said, "So son, what did you do?"

"I gave my heart to Jesus, Dad. I asked him to be my Lord."

"Do you know what you're doing?"

"Yeah, I know what I'm doing."

It was a great day, we rejoiced and partied all day about it. And then when he got baptized, we were so thrilled. They've got a really good marriage, and they've got two wonderful kids, we have a grandson and a granddaughter, and it's powerful.

Here's another short story about how high Colleen set the bar, but it also shows she was feisty, she had a hot temper. I actually loved it, although I was the brunt of it sometimes. One time, we were going on a trip to visit her mom in Saint George, Utah. We were on our way, but we were late, and I swear to this, it was her that made us late, but I won't go there.

Anyway, we were arguing about being late, I mean we fussed at each other, I'm Scottish and hot-tempered and stubborn, and she's Irish and hot-tempered and stubborn. So we were having this little fight, and I was being a jerk, driving up the freeway about 90 miles an hour, weaving in and out of traffic.

"Slow down; you're gonna kill us," she said. "Quit weaving in and out."

I was stubborn; I was stupid; I look back on it now, and I was absolutely an idiot.

"I have to go to the bathroom," she said. "There's a Target up the road."

"Okay." So I pulled off the freeway, and I was mad. "You better hurry!" I said.

I parked right in front of the curb, because usually in a Target store the bathroom's right at the front door, and so she went in while I sat in the car revving the engine.

A few minutes later, she walked out of the Target, and instead of getting in the car, she just started walking down the sidewalk.

I rolled down the window and drove alongside her. "Colleen, get into the car."

She just kept walking.

I got more and more upset. "Colleen! Get your butt in the car!"

She kept walking.

Butt turned into the word *ass*. I said, "Set your ass down in the car! We're running late!"

She walked right out in front of the car and out into the parking lot. There weren't many cars, so I just drove beside her.

"Get in the car!"

Finally, she stopped. She leaned down and looked in the car window. "If you were a man of God, you'd turn off that car, you'd come around and put your arms around me, and you would pray."

Well, I felt about a quarter of an inch high. Exasperated, I put the car in park, turned off the engine, pulled out the key, got out, put my arms around her and I started to pray.

At first, I was praying, "Lord, make this woman not be so

stubborn," but that quickly turned into realizing I was a jerk, so I asked God to forgive me for being a jerk. That I love my wife, and I'm sorry, I shouldn't have been such a jerk, and I'm sorry I scared her, and I asked that the Lord would come in and touch my heart. Take this evil spirit that's trying to rob us of joy.

And finally, at the end of the prayer she just looked up at me and smiled, gave me a pretty little kiss and then she said, "That's better isn't it?"

"Yeah, that's better."

"Now hand me the keys and get in the car."

She drove the rest of the way.

CHAPTER 10

You know the basics of the last part of our story, but I guess I should tell you the details. We were on vacation, headed to Tulsa to visit our son. We flew into Tulsa, and we spent a week with him, our daughter, and their two kids.

Oh, Nana was in heaven. Colleen was so excited to play with the girls.

Our two little beautiful granddaughters, Katie Joy and Ellie Ray, were all over Colleen, and she loved every minute. She was on the floor playing with them; it was just a sight to see. And after she stood up they lifted their arms; they wanted to be held. And they didn't seem to want to do anything with Papa—they tried to do everything with Nana, and she just ate it up. She had the best time.

Inevitably, it came time to leave; we left on Monday and headed over to Arkansas to see some friends; they met us halfway, and we had lunch together and had a great time of fellowship and fun and laughing and eating, it was great.

From there, it was about a seven-hour trip down to Waco, and another half-hour to the ranch south of Waco where I grew up. We were going to surprise our cousins and stop and see them; plus, Colleen hadn't ever been to the ranch, and I was excited for her to see it. There's not much left of the ranch—thirty, forty acres—but it was going to be fun. My family's a really fun family, and I love them a lot, so I thought, *Well, this'll be fun.*

It was supposed to be a seven-hour drive, but we made it last two days. I mean, we were already having so much fun. We were laughing and having the best time. It was wonderful.

We stayed overnight in Hillsboro, Texas, about thirty miles north of Waco. The next morning Colleen wasn't feeling well, and I thought maybe it's because we've been sleeping in strange beds and spending hours in the car. So I said, "Why don't we just lay low today? We're not in a big-time hurry; we're okay. We'll take it easy; I'll get some food, we'll watch TV, and rest."

"Oh, that'll be good," she said. So we did just that, but she was still really sore. She took a shower, came out, and just felt terrible.

We sat there and watched TV, and she laid there, moaning and writhing. I gave her some Advil for the pain and then she said, "I need to go to the bathroom."

I helped her into the bathroom, and she said, "Don't leave. I feel dizzy."

She never did that. We'd been married thirty-four years, and she'd never once asked me to stay in the bathroom while she used it.

So I stayed, and then helped her back into bed, and as I looked at her face, she did not look good at all. Her eyes looked terrible, her skin looked awful, she looked sick. I'd never seen her look like that before.

"Honey," I said, "I'm going to take you to the ER. Let me get you dressed."

"No, just leave me in my pajamas," she said. She would never, ever go out in her pajamas, so now I knew for sure there was a problem.

The whole time we were married, if I ever asked her how she was feeling and she felt terrible, she'd say "Pretty so-so." She never complained, never. About anything. Never.

So I hurried and rushed her to an emergency room across the freeway. We got her in quickly to the building, and she told me as we were walking in, "Tell them it's my heart, maybe if they think I'm having a heart attack, they'll get me in right away."

She never lied, so that was just real unusual of her to say that. It made me see that she knew she was really sick.

They took a look at her right away and said her blood pressure was very low and her oxygen level was about 70 (it should be at 100). They said she was in really bad shape and that it looked like a growth in her lung, or at least they thought it was in her lung, so they ordered an x-ray to check it. She wasn't breathing very well.

The doctor pulled me aside and asked if Colleen had an advance directive or any of that stuff, to which I replied no.

"What would be your wishes?" he asked.

"What do you mean?"

"If she goes, do you want me to bring her back?"

"What do you mean, 'If she goes?'"

He looked me in the eye. "She may not make it," he said. "This is a small hospital; it's just an ER. We have to transfer her to an ICU in Waco, and I don't know if she's going to make it. If I don't intubate her, she's not going to make it. And I need to start her on these heavy pressure medicines, that'll rob the blood from her fingers and her toes, but if we don't get her blood pressure up, she's not going to make it."

And so I looked at Colleen, and I said, "They say you won't make it if I don't get you intubated."

"I don't want to do that," she said

"I don't either."

"There is no choice," the doctor said. "She will not make it if you don't do that."

So I looked at her, and she said, "Okay, let's go for it."

"Let's just trust God," I said. And so I prayed with her and then they intubated her. They also had to give her sedatives, so she was out of it.

Then they put her in the ambulance, and it was a little one—too small for me to ride along. So I grabbed her stuff, jumped in the car, and followed the ambulance, right on their bumper. Eighty, ninety miles an hour down the road I'm following that ambulance, I'm four feet behind the ambulance. And I'm watching through the back window as the ambulance guy, the EMT or whatever he was, worked on her.

It was the longest, hardest drive I ever made.

I called my kids and told them what was going on. I didn't want the kids to panic, but I knew this was serious, I mean they said she might not make it.

Then when the ambulance got close to the hospital in Waco, they turned on the sirens and the lights. They hadn't had those on while they were on the freeway, so now I panicked. I thought she was in distress, but I found out later it's a protocol to let the ER know they're coming in.

At first, they wouldn't let me back to see her, but when I got back to see her, she was out of it on the sedative. But she was stable.

I didn't know where we were headed.

The doctors fought for her. They put her on dialysis because her body was building up fluid and her kidneys weren't working, and she was on dialysis for seven days, twenty-four hours a day. Her kidneys never did kick back in, and then when you're on dialysis it drops your blood pressure, so then they have to up the pressure medicine.

Her feet started turning black first; then her fingers began turning black. And I don't even know if I want to tell you about that. It's so hard.

Let's say it was two weeks—fifteen days, to be exact—of living hell.

Watching her go was the hardest thing I've ever done in my life.

We have a gazebo in the back of our house, and Colleen and I liked sitting in it in the evening. We'd watch the sunset; I'd get my guitar and sing love songs to her. I haven't dared to sit in that gazebo since she passed. I will again someday, I hope.

One night as we were sitting in our gazebo—it was only a few months ago—she said, "I need you to make me a promise."

"Okay."

"I want you to promise you'll let me die first."

Oh, who could decide a thing like that! I mean, that's not up to me, that's God's call. I'd had open heart surgery, and a stent of carotid artery surgery, I mean, I'm a mess. I'm seven years older than she is, so I'm thinking, *There's no way you're going to go before me.*

But I never told her no about anything.

So I said, "Okay, I promise I'll let you go first."

Never dreaming she would.

Never dreaming it would be her.

Another night we were sitting in the gazebo and Colleen said, "We don't have a retirement plan, we live by whatever offerings come in the door. We live from day to day, and that's how we've been living for almost thirty years. And it's been great, but there's not a retirement plan."

And I'm singing to her, and she said, "Honey, what are we going to do when you're too old to sing?"

"Well, I don't know," I said. And then I remembered a Scripture. "You know Psalm 37:4."

She knew it. "Delight in the Lord, and He'll give you the desires of your heart."

"I think as long as we keep delighting in our Lord," I said, "and keep our eyes on Him and keep seeking Him first, I don't think we have to worry about it. He'll lead us to green pastures and still waters."

And that seemed to satisfy both of us, so we just sat there and looked at the sunset.

I was watching Colleen's sunset. No more retirement plan. And how was I supposed to delight in the Lord right now? I was watching her go, and her blood pressure kept dropping. Her breathing was shallow, so they put her on a CPAP machine, but it didn't work and they had to intubate her again.

I was watching her go, the kids were standing there with me, and I leaned down and kissed her little face.

She was so soft, so warm.

She was sedated, so I don't know, I guess she knew what I was doing. I don't know.

"Honey, I can't fix this," I said. "This is one thing I can't fix. But I'm keeping my promise. You can go first. But you have to wait for me."

Then I thought of something she'd said to me just a few weeks earlier.

"Sam Parsons, if I die first, you have to promise me you'll never leave the sanctuary. That you'll serve God with all your heart until you come to be with me in heaven.

"Don't leave the sanctuary, honey."

Gosh.

So my last words to her were a promise. "I'll be in the sanctuary. I'll serve God."

And that's what I'm still trying to do.

May 10th, 2018 was her day.

Psalm 139:16 says this: "Your eyes saw me when I was in the womb, and all the days ordained for me are recorded in your scroll before one of them came into existence."

May 10th, 2018 was Colleen's day.

I don't know when my day is.

I just got diagnosed with pancreatic cancer. The doctor gives me about six months to live, though if I do chemo, he said I can maybe extend my life a couple of years.

My kids want me to do chemo.

I don't.

It's not that I want to hurry home to Colleen, although that's the truth, I do. I feel like I need to be in the sanctuary and I need strength, and I think that chemo will rob my strength. And I think the day of my death is marked already. The doctor can't give me—he's a nice guy, a great doctor—but he can't give me any more time than God has allotted for me.

And so, Colleen, I'll keep my promise. That you go first, and I will stay in the sanctuary. And I will serve God with all my heart.

Oh, but I miss you so.

I fell in love with Colleen Parsons when she was Colleen McCune. She was the most beautiful thing I ever laid eyes on, and every season of her life she was the most beautiful thing I ever saw. I loved her with all my heart.

I still love her with all my heart, forever and ever, amen.

When we said our vows, "Till death do us part," I didn't mean just one dies. For me, I'm a one-woman man, and she's the one woman for me. I thank God and His mercy that He hasn't caused me to come home sooner, but I've still got stuff to do.

I will see her again, I just merely hope the time will be shortened and pass quickly. In the meantime, I have work still to be done. At least I think I do. By the time this book is complete and published and on the shelves, I will have probably already gone into heaven myself.

Until then, I'm going to stay in the sanctuary, and I'm going to praise God for giving me the best wife that ever lived.

My heart is broken, my heart is filled with sorrow, but I will worship You, God.

You give and take away. Blessed be the name of the Lord.

Thank you for giving me the best wife ever.

Oh Colleen, I love you with all of my heart.

The end.

Colleen and Alyssa when
Alyssa was only 1 1/2 years old.

Colleen took this picture of
Alyssa and me on our way to
Tulsa all together.

Colleen and little John, our 5th
grandson. She didn't live long
enough to see Joseph, our last
grandson.

Me and Leen at our kitchen
table...I must have done
something right to get a kiss
like that.

Colleen and I at Nick and Courtney's wedding.

Colleen with our first grandchild Joshua...she sure loved babies!

Our crazy family...we loved to love and laugh a lot!

Colleen with 3-year-old Grace on her back and 4-year-old Joshua under her...the kids loved wrestling with Colleen on the floor and building tents in the dining room.

Our crazy family again!

About the Author

Sam was born April 7, 1949 and was raised on a cattle ranch outside of Waco, Texas. He started his professional music career at the early age of 14 and has performed all over the country in 49 of the 50 states. He has been a recording artist on United Artists as the bass singer for the Four Lads, and later as a single artist on ABC Records. He was a theme writer for Universal Pictures, as well as ghost-writer for Frank Sinatra's production team. He is a versatile musical artist, comfortable in a variety of musical styles. Sam is the composer of over 400 songs, an arranger, recording artist, and live stage performer. He currently sings and speaks to thousands of people each year in a number of interesting venues across the country.

Each week Sam helps direct two Christian men's groups providing the music and training for over 400 men in Orange County, CA. Sam and his wife and Colleen have four children: Alyssa, Travis, Nick, and Tasha, and five grandchildren, Joshua, Grace, Katie Joy, Ellie Rae, and John Samuel. Sam has been in Christian ministry since 1985, with his is first ministry position being the Associate Director of Music for Mission Viejo Christian Church. Later he was the Director of Music for the singles ministry at the Crystal Cathedral in Garden Grove, California. Sam has been on staff at four churches as the Music Director/Worship Leader and has provided worship for a number of conferences and retreats. After much study, Sam became a Senior Pastor in 1992. That same year, Sam and his wife, Colleen stepped out together, in faith, to co-direct a faith-based Christian ministry, Good News Ministry, a non-profit Christian ministry primarily ministering in hospitals, nursing homes, retirement homes, and assisted living facilities. Sam visits hundreds of seniors each month, singing and spreading his contagious joy. He continues to teach Bible studies and occasionally provides pulpit supply for other pastors and worship leaders. He is a strong men's retreat speaker and worship leader and has a number of musical CDs available. Sam's personal mission statement is:

To reach out with the encouragement of God through music and inspirational motivation, striving always to be Biblically sound, and compassionately sensitive.

Made in the USA
Middletown, DE
01 September 2019